Table of Contents

Preparing for Science Journal Writing 2-3

Assessing Science Journals 4

Introducing the Journal to the Class 5

Science Overview 6-9

Plant Life 10-18

Animal Life 19-25

Ecosystems 26-32

Matter, Energy, and Light 33-43

The Solar System, Weather, and
Rocks and Minerals 44-61

Science Review Exercises 62-64

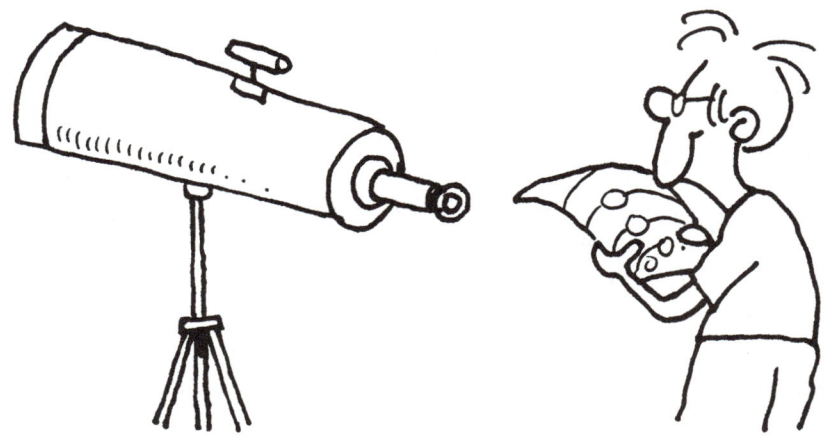

Preparing for Science Journal Writing

Purposes of Science Journals

Science journals serve many functions. Journals are convenient locations to store data and results of experiments. They can lower the frustration level of learning scientific concepts as they ease children into the discovery that science is fun and exciting. Journals can help students see how well they understand science and science concepts, and show teachers each student's strengths and weaknesses. Journal activities also increase students' writing, reasoning, vocabulary, and drawing skills. Data organization, like chart and map making, becomes a learned skill through science journal activities. Above all, journals allow children guided, creative time to experiment, analyze, and learn. The science journal activities in this book can stimulate your students' natural curiosity and creativity, as well as encourage questioning, autonomy, and discovery. Through these learning experiences, children will be more likely to develop a confident and positive attitude toward scientific inquiry and discovery.

Materials Needed

Each student will need a sturdy, bound notebook which has a pocket. Your students can create their own journal books, or you may find it most convenient for them to use spiral notebooks. If a student's journal does not have a pocket to ensure that loose papers will not be lost, you can easily make one. Staple a piece of cardboard (cut to fit to the inside bottom half of the back cover) along the sides and bottom, leaving the top part open.

Students will need various writing and drawing materials as the activities suggest. Let the students label the outside of their notebooks in large, block letters, **Science Journal**, and have them put their names on the covers, as well.

Tell the students that these notebooks are very special as they will contain the students' written and illustrated scientific journeys. If you provide journals for the class, make a presentation that reinforces this idea.

It is helpful and convenient to keep the science journals in a specific place in the room. This will ensure easy access and prevent students from accidentally losing them or using them for other subjects.

Materials other than notebooks are listed for the activities which require some preparation. This way you will have all the supplies the students will need.

Time Allotment

Allow time daily for science journal writing, if possible. Schedule the journal sessions to be at the same time each day, mark it on your calendar, and let the students know when it will be. This will help them look forward to it. You might find that it is an excellent way to close your science period every day.

When you pass out the journals, allow the students to doodle briefly or draw in them. This will help them loosen up and get their minds in a creative mode. Provide a minimum of fifteen minutes for each journal writing session. Because of the nature of some activities, some days you will need more time. Sometimes, you may want or need to spread an activity over a few days.

Teacher Instructions

Before each day's science journal session, be sure you spend some time reading the selected activity and understand how to complete it. Assemble the materials the activity requires (if any), and complete the exercise on your own. Think about the science themes involved, the possible outcomes, and how they apply to your current science studies, as well as to daily life.

Stimulate Thinking with Leading Questions

Another approach to assessing your class's progress in science is to ask the students to respond to one or two of the following questions to begin or end each journal session.

- What topic did you study in science today?

- What did you learn about science today?

- What did you like best in science today? What did you like least?

- How would you describe today's lesson to a friend who is absent today?

- What problems did you have with your science homework?

- What questions do you have about today's lesson or assignment?

Activity Boxes

Look through the student-directed activities (enclosed in boxes) on pages 6 through 55 to find the ones that are most appropriate to your current studies. Initially, guide the students as they complete the exercises. Later, after the students are accustomed to writing in their journals and responding to the prompts, you may want to put the ideas relating to the unit you are currently studying on cards, laminate them, and let each student draw an activity from the pile. Remind the students that the bold sentences on the cards should have written responses in their journals. If a student draws a card he has already completed, have him draw again. This approach can further enhance student autonomy. Later, the students may want to create their own cards.

Supplementary Activities

The supplementary activities at the end of each section are designed for the entire class to do together, with the teacher supervising and guiding the students through the steps. Group work can foster skills such as cooperation and leadership. Students can learn how to cooperate and combine their knowledge and personal strengths with those of other group members to attain certain goals. Also, your students can develop a sense of community as they explore science together.

© Carson-Dellosa Publ. CD-7317 *Teacher Instructions*

Assessing Science Journals

Evaluation of Student Participation

Science journals can help you evaluate the level of knowledge and understanding of concepts your students have regarding science. Do not treat the science journals as regular assignments that require grading, as that could make the class dread them. Instead of employing traditional evaluation methods, such as tests and research papers, ask the students to share what they have recorded from time to time, either individually, with the whole class, or in small groups.

Ask the children what they are learning about themselves, what they are learning about science, and what they are learning about the world around them as they work through activities. They can either respond orally or write their responses to these questions in their journals. Another alternative is to have the students answer these questions on separate sheets of paper to be turned in to you.

Check the students' journals periodically to make sure that they are completing the journal activities you assign. You could randomly choose different students each day to share what is in their journals with you. This type of evaluation can serve several functions. It can provide one-on-one contact with the students and a more in-depth look at each student's writing, progress, and questions. It can also motivate the students to complete the activities as they are assigned. Students will never know when their journals may be chosen for review!

Teacher Convenience and Utility

Science journal writing encourages students to engage in a self-discovery process of scientific understanding. These activities do not require complicated lesson plans nor do they create piles of papers to grade and correct, leaving teachers with more time and energy to guide students on the path of scientific knowledge. This book also includes many activities which require students to do research. These activities could be springboards for further study or critical thinking.

Teacher Instructions

Introducing Science Journals to the Class

Guiding Science Journal Writing

As you lead the children through the science journal ideas and activities in this book, ask the students leading questions to help guide them and to encourage independent thinking. The following question formats can spark students' thinking and help them make their own discoveries. If at all possible, avoid asking questions that require simple *Yes* or *No* answers. While yes or no responses can help focus the class on your discussion, they may not encourage critical thinking.

- What do you think would happen if. . .

- Why do you think something is not working? How could you change it to make it work?

- Why do you think something happened?

- How has something changed?

- How would your life (or the world) be different if. . .

The Scientific Method

The scientific method is the set of logical steps that scientists follow when they try to find factual answers to their questions. Show the class a chart of the scientific method or make your own chart by listing the steps below. Explain to your students that they are to employ these steps in all their science experiments as this method forms the foundation for scientific discovery. Discuss what is done in each step.

Step 1	**Purpose**—Decide what it is you want to learn.
Step 2	**Research**—Find out as much as you can about your topic.
Step 3	**Hypothesis**—Predict the answer to the problem.
Step 4	**Experiment**—Design a test to confirm or disprove your hypothesis.
Step 5	**Analysis**—Record what happened during the experiment.
Step 6	**Conclusion**—State why your hypothesis was correct or incorrect.

Science Overview

The Activity Boxes in this section can motivate your students to learn more about the world of science. By analyzing the daily impact science has on their lives, students can realize the importance of exploring scientific concepts. (Refer to page 3 for instructions on using these activities.)

Science Learning Styles

People have different styles of learning, and science is one subject that can be shaped to fit almost everyone's approach to learning. Read the following methods and think about which method is your favorite way to learn.

1. **Observation**—Some people learn by watching other people do something and then doing it themselves.
2. **Read and Do**—Some people learn by reading about how to do something and then trying it themselves.
3. **Visual Instructions**—Some people prefer to follow steps that are drawn out in pictures.
4. **Solo or with a Partner**—Some people prefer to work alone, while others like to work with a classmate.

Use your journal to write about how you learn science best. What can your teacher do to make it more fun for you to learn science?

Checking in with Yourself

Your feelings are important. They affect your schoolwork and your friendships. Check in with your feelings right now. How do you feel? Why? The way you feel about science affects how well you do in it. Some days you might like science better than other days. How do you feel about science today?

In your journal, complete the sentence that is true for you today. If both are true, complete both sentences.

I like science today because . . .   **I dislike science today because . . .**

The Importance of Science

Why is it important to learn about science? Do you think studying science is important? Why or why not?

Write in your journal about science and its importance in life. Tell how you feel about science and how you feel when you learn something new about science.

Science in Daily Life

How is science used in daily life? Think about planning and cooking meals, using energy for transportation and communication, caring for yourself, growing plants, and other aspects of life. How can you benefit by knowing more about these things?

Think about some dangerous aspects of life. Why is it important to know which ingredients are poisonous and which are not? What chemical reactions can cause problems? Can you name any such combinations?

In your journal, write about why it is important to understand scientific concepts and theories.

What Is a Scientist?

List the things that come to mind when you hear the word *scientist*. **In your journal, draw a picture of the type of scientist you might be interested in being. Show the tools used in this profession.**

Write a paragraph in your journal about your scientist, telling what he or she does. How are you like the scientist and how are you different? What is the best thing about being the type of scientist you have drawn?

What I Don't Understand Is . . .

Science is great for people who ask questions, because science tries to explain everything. What science concept or idea do you not understand? What confuses you about your current science studies?

If you could ask anything about science that you wanted, what would you ask? Pretend you are the only student in class. **Write a note to your teacher asking any question about science.** Ask questions about things you don't understand or things you want to learn.

Hand these questions in to your teacher. Ask your teacher to respond to your questions either orally or in writing. Store the written response in your journal or write a summary of your teacher's oral response.

© Carson-Dellosa Publ. CD-7317

Science Overview

Science Overview Supplementary Activities

Science Safety Bulletin Board

Before children begin working on science projects, they need to be reminded of science safety rules. Have the students help you make a Science Safety bulletin board to reinforce good safety practices. First, have them suggest safety rules and procedures (recommendations follow), then **make a safety checklist** for the bulletin board by writing the rules on a large piece of colored poster board. Attach the poster board to the bulletin board when completed. **Ask the class to make a banner for the bulletin board with a slogan that promotes science safety.** The letters needed for the banner could be cut from various colors of construction paper and stapled to the bulletin board or simply written in black marker on a long strip of white paper and attached to the top of the bulletin board.

Ask the students to draw and cut out science safety gear pictures to display on the bulletin board. They could draw goggles and safety glasses, aprons, gloves, soap and water, etc. Other items that would be appropriate for the bulletin board are measuring devices, such as a balance, measuring cups, and so on.

Before beginning science experiments, have the students review the safety rules so all students will have science safety in mind before they begin their work. **The students can make a notebook-sized copy of the rules to keep in their journals. Laminate their copies so they can check off the items in the list each time they participate in a project.** Some ideas for your list follow:

1. Measure and follow the steps of the experiment carefully.
2. Listen carefully to all of the teacher's directions.
3. Wash your hands before and after performing an experiment or handling materials.
4. Wear gloves, safety goggles, and aprons when needed.
5. Dispose of waste properly.
6. Clean up your work area.
7. Do not run or play in the classroom lab.
8. Be careful with objects that are hot, made of glass, or sharp. Use hot pads when needed. If something breaks, do not move, and have someone notify the teacher immediately.
9. Do not smell or taste anything in the experiment unless the teacher says it is okay.

Career Counselors

Have the students pretend to be career counselors who help people learn about job opportunities in the field of science. Let each student decide the area of science in which he is most interested, and let him be a counselor for that area. If two or more students are interested in the same area, try to have them further define their interests so they will not report on the same exact jobs. For instance, students interested in animals may decide to counsel on careers as veterinarians for pets, large animals, zoos, or wild animals; as zoologists interested in field work or research; as biologists interested in marine, fresh water, forest, or desert habitats; as entomologists; as wildlife conservationists; as park rangers, forest rangers, game wardens, or lake wardens; and so on.

1. **Tell the students to research their choices using the library and other available resources.** Encourage students to call local professionals in the chosen fields and local government employment offices for more information. Have students find out what education the positions require, the areas of the country or world in which the positions are commonly available, the salary ranges, the responsibilities of the positions, and so on. **They can enter the information in their science journals.**

2. **Let the students create brochures to display their information.** They should try to make the brochures look and sound professional. Students should inform people about the career opportunities as well as make the positions sound exciting. Tell students to use illustrations or photographs from magazines and other sources to decorate their brochures.

3. **Hold a career day when the students can pretend they do the jobs they researched.** Set up a table at which they can make presentations. Encourage students to dress for their part and to make props and posters. Each student should talk about the career opportunities in the area of science he selected, show his brochure, and show any other props he has. Let each student make a presentation, and allow the class to have a question-and-answer session after each presentation.

Plant Life

The Activity Boxes in this section will accent your students' studies of plant life as they grow and care for plants, explore plant communities, compare and contrast different types of plants, and so on. Remind the students that plants are living organisms.

Life Cycles

Many different types of plants follow similar life cycles. Choose a plant to track through its life cycle. **Read about it and diagram its life cycle in your journal, beginning with its seed stage.** Include seed dispersal, germination, growth patterns, and the plant's creation of new seeds. How does the plant replenish the soil after taking in its nutrients? Include this in your diagram.

Write a paragraph that identifies your plant and explains the steps of its life cycle.

Petals, Stamens, and Sepals

Draw a flower and label its parts. Think about how the flower is pollinated and how its seeds are formed.

Write a story in your journal that tells how a butterfly, bee, or hummingbird helps flowers make their seeds. Tell how plants, insects, and animals are dependent on each other. What would happen if the insects and animals didn't help the plant?

I Just Ate a Flower!

When we eat vegetables, we eat different parts of plants. Broccoli makes up the flower and stem of the plant. We eat celery stems and leaves. The potatoes that we turn into chips and fries come from the tuber root of the potato plant.

In your journal, make a chart with *leaves, stems, roots, fruits,* and *flowers* as the headings. List at least ten different vegetables and find out what parts of the plant they are. Do not include the vegetables used as examples above in your list. Write the vegetables from your list under the correct headings on your chart. If a vegetable belongs in more than one category, list it under each heading that applies.

"Magic" Beans teacher directions—Each student will need two or three beans; two small, clear plastic cups; cotton balls; water; and masking tape to begin the "Magic" Beans experiment below. Provide the freshest beans possible, perhaps from a natural food store. Try lima, lentil, or navy beans, or let the students try some of each type.

The students will design their own experiments, but the following information can provide some guidelines if they get stumped. Have each student wet a cotton ball, squeeze out the excess water, and put it in the bottom of one cup. The cotton should cover the entire bottom of the cup and begin to spread up the cup's sides. Let each student then put two or three beans, spaced an equal distance apart, between the cotton and the sides of the cup. Tell each student to tape the mouth of the second cup to the mouth of the first cup. Keep the cups away from direct sunlight and extreme heat or cold. The beans should sprout and grow in three days to a week. Students should check the seeds daily while waiting for them to sprout. Put the sprouts in filtered sunlight when green leaves appear. To continue the test, the children can transplant the sprouts into dirt in larger cups or small pots.

"Magic" Beans

Read the story of "Jack and the Beanstalk." **Test real beans to see how they compare to the magic beans in the story. Write out your hypothesis and design an experiment.** List the materials you use and the steps of the test. In the experiment, grow some beans in a clear plastic cup. Plot their growth on a chart in your journal.

Write your conclusion to the experiment in your journal, describing the differences between the growth of your beans and Jack's magic beans.

If I Could Be a Plant...

Think of all that you know about plants. Consider the different adaptations various plants have made to suit their environments. Think about the ways similar plants such as trees can also be different: some trees have broad leaves while others have thin leaves called needles. Some plants, such as wildflowers, do not produce food for people, while others, like vegetable plants, do. If you could be a plant, what would you be, and why? **Write your responses in your journal, and draw a picture of yourself as that plant.**

Seed Hunt

Go on a seed hunt! Search for seeds inside as many fruits as possible. Fruits you could include in your seed hunt are apples, pears, peaches, oranges, grapefruits, seeded grapes, cantaloupes, honeydew melons, bananas, and plums.

In your journal, record where you found each seed, how many seeds you found, and the size and shape of the seeds. Draw a sample of each seed. Compare the seeds from each fruit in a few sentences. How are they all alike? How are they different?

Seed Anatomy teacher directions—For the Seed Anatomy activity below, provide students with corn kernels and fresh bean seeds (such as lentils, lima beans, or navy beans). Soak the bean seeds overnight. Show the students how to pull the seeds apart at the split. When the students examine the seeds' halves, point out that bean seeds are classified as *dicots* and possess two *cotyledons* (structures that provide food and serve as the seed's "leaves"), whereas corn kernels are classed as *monocots* and have only one cotyledon. Provide a diagram of a monocot and dicot for the students. Help the students locate the *pericarp, endosperm,* and *cotyledon* of the corn kernel and the *seed coat, cotyledon, plumule, micropyle,* and *hilum* on the bean seed.

Seed Anatomy

What is the difference between seeds classified as *monocots* and *dicots*? Look the terms up in a dictionary, encyclopedia, or biology book.

Slip off the seed coat from a soaked bean seed. Carefully pull apart the bean seed's cotyledons (the two halves of the seeds that together give the seed food). What do you see inside? Examine a corn kernel and see if you can determine how it differs from the bean seed.

Draw pictures of both the bean seed and the corn kernel. Label their parts, define the terms *monocot* and *dicot*, and give two examples of each.

Deciduous and Coniferous Trees

In an encyclopedia or science book, look up the definitions for the terms *deciduous* and *coniferous*. **Write the definitions in your journal along with a few sentences comparing and contrasting deciduous and coniferous trees.** How are they similar? How are they different? **Draw and label pictures to help show the differences.**

Pretend that you are a deciduous or a coniferous tree and write a letter to your pen pal, who is the other type of tree. (If you choose to be coniferous, your pen pal will be a deciduous tree, for example.) Tell your pen pal about your life. Include such things as how you look, what you do from season to season, the types of animals that live in or near you, and other things about your life. Share your letter with a classmate who wrote from the other point of view.

Tree Bark

Read about tree bark in a science book. **In your journal, list the purposes of tree bark.** Research the many ways the bark helps the tree live. How does it hurt a tree when people carve their initials into its bark or pound in nails for tree houses?

Write a story about a tree that has smooth bark, such as a birch tree. Tell what happens to the tree when someone carves in its bark or builds a tree house in its branches. Imagine how the tree might feel. What happens to it?

A Cactus and a Fir Tree

Read about cacti and fir trees in an encyclopedia or science book, then write a few paragraphs in your journal describing what is similar and different about them. Tell what they need to grow and where they grow in nature. Explain how a cactus's leaves help it, and compare a cactus's leaves with a fir tree's leaves. **Write about the adaptations that both have made to live in their very different environments.** If you could be either a cactus or a fir tree, which would you be? Why?

Description Drawings

Much of the time, humans rely on the sense of sight to gather information about the world. In this activity, you will try drawing something you have not seen as someone describes it. This experience can show you how other senses can help us "see."

Pick a partner. Go on a walk, but do not walk together. Each of you needs to collect a few nature objects, such as leaves, flowers, bark, and so on. Put the objects in a paper bag so your partner will not see them.

When you and your partner return to the classroom, get your journals and the bags of nature items. Sit on the floor with your back against your partner's back. Take one object from your bag and tell your partner to try to draw it as you describe it. Do not tell what it is, but describe the color, size, shape, texture, and thickness of your object to your partner. Pretend you have never before seen your object, and notice all the special things about it. For example, is it smooth all over, or are there lumpy places or crevices on it?

After your partner has finished the drawing, switch roles. Let your partner describe one of his or her objects as you draw it. When you are done, show each other the objects you described and see how closely your pictures match. Try this activity again, using different objects.

Write your responses and reactions to the activity in your journal. The second time you helped your partner, how did your descriptions change? How were you better able to guide your partner this time? Did you listen differently the second time you drew? How did you understand how to turn what you heard into a picture? How will you begin to look at things differently now?

Symbiosis

Find out what *symbiosis* means by looking up the word in a dictionary. *Lichen* is a good example of a symbiotic plant. Read about lichen in your science book or in a book about plants.

Lichen is found all over the world. It is made of two different types of plants living together, an *algae* and a *fungus*. **In your journal, take notes about lichen, describing what each plant gives to the relationship and the different circumstances under which lichen can live. Explain how lichen is an example of symbiosis. Look for some examples of lichen outside or find a picture of it in a science book, and draw what you see in your journal.**

Plant Life — 14 — © Carson-Dellosa Publ. CD-7317

Plant Communities teacher directions—For the Plant Communities activity below, the students can use any enclosed clear glass or plastic containers to make terrariums.

Have students put a 1" layer of sand or gravel, mixed with charcoal, in the bottom of the container as a drainage layer. Charcoal (sold at pet supply stores) helps keep the terrarium fresh because it helps prevent mildew. Small pieces of broken clay flower pots can also be added to the drainage layer, if desired. Next, the students should add a 2" layer of potting soil on top of the drainage layer.

Provide the class with a broad selection of small plants (your local garden supply store may be able to make recommendations). Some species of wild woodland plants may be available from a scientific supply company or florist, or the students could use different varieties of house plants. Have the students collect the soil, worms, and other items that are part of the plants' habitat. The students should make holes in the soil layer for the plants, insert the plants carefully, and press the soil firmly around them. Use a plant mister or atomizer to water the plants. Wet the plants and soil well, but be careful not to make the soil soggy.

Put the glass cover on the terrarium container and place it where the plants can get indirect light. Do not place the terrarium in direct sunlight.

Plant Communities

How do the plants in an ecosystem help each other? Some plants may be tall and shield smaller plants from intense sunlight, for example. Host trees provide support for clinging vines. Often, moss and lichen form symbiotic relationships with trees and other plants. Think of other beneficial relationships plants establish for one another in an ecosystem.

Make a *terrarium* to study one plant community. Follow the directions given by your teacher. Select several small plants from the varieties provided by your teacher. Note if the plant has any information listed on a tag or on its container. Usually, these tags tell whether the plant prefers sun or shade, how tall the plant will grow, etc. Decide where each plant should be placed in the terrarium.

In your journal, draw a diagram that shows where each plant will go. Make a chart on another page in your journal and keep a record of how quickly each plant grows. Place the terrarium near a window so all the plants get an adequate amount of light, but do not place the terrarium in direct sunlight.

© Carson-Dellosa Publ. CD-7317 *Plant Life*

Leafy "Tree"-Shirts teacher directions—For the Leafy "Tree"-Shirts activity below, provide your students with fabric paints (obtained at a craft store) or acrylic paints to decorate t-shirts they have brought from home. Fabric paints hold up well in the wash, but to ensure the permanence of acrylic paints, you may choose to coat the shirts with fixative, also available at craft stores. Bring in newspapers and cardboard. Students should wear smocks to protect their clothing.

Leafy "Tree"- Shirts

Nature can be seen as an interesting and beautiful mixture of textures and colors. Put a bit of nature on a "tree"-shirt. You will need a light-colored, plain cotton t-shirt (an old one works fine).

Go on a nature walk and collect different tree leaves and twigs which have fallen on the ground. In the classroom, arrange the leaves and twigs on newspapers on the floor to create a nice design to put on your t-shirt. Put some cardboard inside the t-shirt and lay it flat on more newspapers.

Lightly coat one side of a leaf or twig with paint and lay it, paint side down, on your shirt where you want it to go. Put a scrap piece of plain paper over the leaf and press it firmly to transfer the paint from the leaf to the t-shirt. Carefully lift off the paper and the leaf, and do not touch the paint on the shirt until it is dry. Repeat with all your leaves and twigs until your nature design is completed.

Write in your journal about the prints you made on your "tree"-shirt. Describe the colors and textures of the trees that you saw and how they are reflected in your shirt design.

Making Gifts of Nature

Make a gift of nature to give to someone special. First, go on a nature walk with your class and collect some leaves and flowers that you think are pretty.

In the classroom, try to identify the leaves and flowers by using some plant identification books from the library. Sketch the nature items and record their names in your journal.

Next, prepare the items for drying by cutting the stems so they are no longer than six inches. Arrange the flowers and leaves on a thick layer of newspaper. On top of the flowers and leaves, place more newspapers, a piece of cardboard, and several heavy books. Leave the items undisturbed for at least one week. Mark the calendar so you will know when to uncover them.

When the flowers and leaves are dried, uncover them. Glue them to thin sheets of tagboard to make bookmarks, or glue them to larger sheets of tagboard to make note cards. **In your journal, write the rough draft for a poem about the flowers and leaves. Write the final draft of your poem on your bookmark or note card.** Place the bookmark or note card between sheets of waxed paper and let your teacher press it lightly with a warm iron. Trim off the excess waxed paper and give the bookmarks or cards as gifts to friends or family members.

Plant Life

Plant Life Supplementary Activities

Fruit Dissection

Help students identify the different parts of seeds and fruits in relation to a plant's life cycle. Bring in an assortment of fresh fruits and a clean, sharp knife. Some fruits to include are apples and peaches (shown below). Since the students may be eating the fruit or using it in the other activities below, make sure the fruit has been washed and dried with paper towels before beginning.

Cover the work surface with layers of absorbent paper. Cut cross sections of the fruit and ask the class to identify the different parts, such as sepals, epidermis, seeds, etc. The diagrams below may help you with this activity. **Have the students diagram the different fruits and label the parts in their journals.** Once the activity is completed, you may want to let the children eat their "dissected" fruit or you can use it for the activity below.

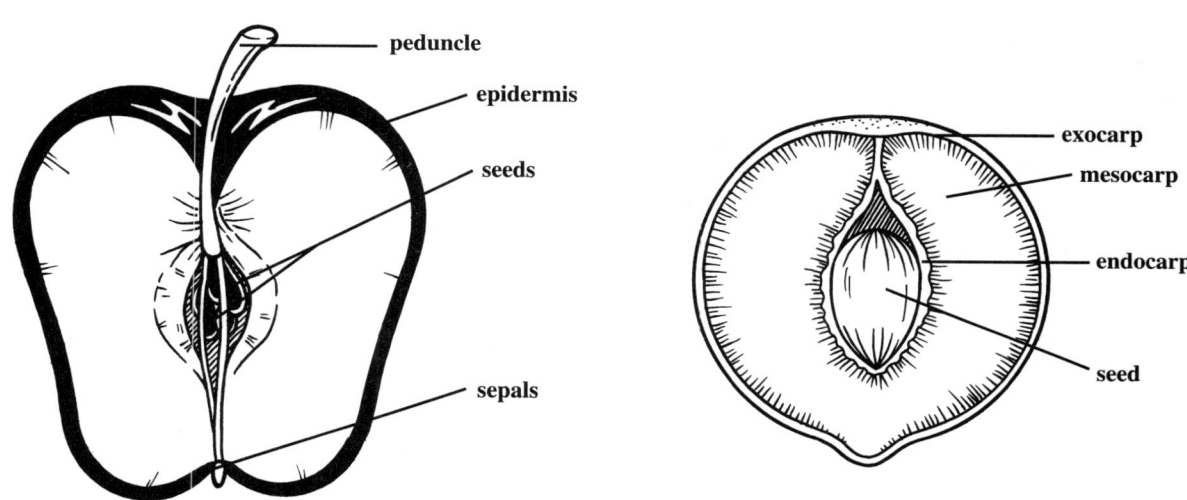

Water Percentage in Fruit

Students can determine what percentage of fruit is water. In addition to the fruit slices above, you need a toaster oven and a small scale (such as a dieter's scale) to complete this activity. Have the students weigh the fruit slices. Treat the slices of one apple (or one peach, etc.) as a unit and weigh them together. **Have the students record the weight of the apple slices and the peach slices in their journals.** Preheat the toaster oven to 160°F and place the fruit, cut side up, on the oven tray. Allow the fruit to dry in the toaster oven for 2 to 6 hours, until the water in the fruit has evaporated. Have the students weigh the pieces of fruit again and record the new weights in their journals.

Before doing the calculations to determine the percentage of water in each type of fruit, ask the students to predict which type contained the most water. Why did they pick that type? **Ask them to write their predictions and reasons for their choices in their journals.** To calculate the percentage of water, subtract the dried fruit weight from the original fruit weight. This equals the weight of the water. Divide the weight of the water by the original fruit weight and multiply by 100 to get the water percentage. Which fruit has the most water? Did the students guess the correct answer? **Have the students record the results in their journals.** Discuss some reasons why dried fruit is useful (weighs less, preserves fruit for areas that might not have fresh fruit, etc.).

Flower Power

A. Find the hidden meanings of flowers. Certain types of flowers attract birds and insects because of their colors and fragrances. Humans can be attracted to flowers for these same reasons, and over the years have even attached special meanings to particular flowers. Ask the students to research flowers as symbols, such as red roses for love, etc., and write the meaning on sentence strips. The list below may help, although some flowers (or herbs) may have more than one symbolic meaning. Have the students draw and color pictures of the flowers. Post the flower pictures and the sentence strips on a bulletin board. **Ask the students to write what their favorite flower is and what meaning they associate with it in their journals.**

Aloe – Healing, protection, affection
Aster – Love
Bachelor's Buttons – Blessedness
Basil – Good wishes, love
Bay – Glory
Carnation – Alas for my poor heart!
Chives – Usefulness
Chrysanthemum, White – Truth
Coriander – Hidden worth
Cumin – Fidelity
Fennel – Flattery
Fern – Sincerity
Forget-me-not – Memories
Gardenia – Secret love
Goldenrod – Encouragement
Holly – Hope
Ivy – Unity, friendship, continuity
Lavender – Devotion, virtue
Lily of the Valley – You've made my life complete.
Lily, Calla – Beauty
Mint – Eternal refreshment
Morning Glory – Affection
Orchid – Refinement
Oregano – Substance
Pansy – Thoughts
Parsley – Festivity
Peony – Happy marriage
Poppy, Red – Consolation
Rose, Pink – Perfect happiness
Rose, Red – Love
Rose, White – Purity
Rose, Yellow – Friendship
Sage – Wisdom, immortality
Zinnia – Lasting affection

B. Have the students find out what different types of flowers they could plant to attract butterflies or hummingbirds. Why are hummingbirds or butterflies attracted to these specific plants? Is it because of a particular scent, color, shape, etc.? **Have students write the results of this research in their science journals.**

C. Explore the medicinal value of plants and herbs. Folk and Native American remedies were often made from commonly found plants, and many of today's medicines can trace their origins back to plants (digitalis, aspirin, etc.). Have the students research plant-based medicines and present the information they find to the rest of the class. **Tell the students to include a copy of the information in their science journals.**

D. Be a floral designer! Divide the children into small groups and give each group a card with an event listed on it that may call for flowers, such as a wedding, a relative's birthday, etc. **Ask the students to use the list of symbolic meanings above (and any other meanings they discover through their research) and to draw a flower arrangement in their science journals.** It may help the students to see pictures of flowers as they are planning their arrangements. Pictures of the varieties listed above could likely be found in gardening or seed catalogs. **The students should list the types of plants they would include in their arrangement in their science journals.** For example, a wedding bouquet may include asters, pink roses, lavender, and ivy. **Ask the students to color their floral arrangement drawings and to label the different types of flowers that are pictured.**

Plant Life

Animal Life

The Activity Boxes in this section can complement your students' explorations of animal life. These activities are designed to guide the class to a deeper understanding of the classification, habitats, characteristics, and other aspects of animal life.

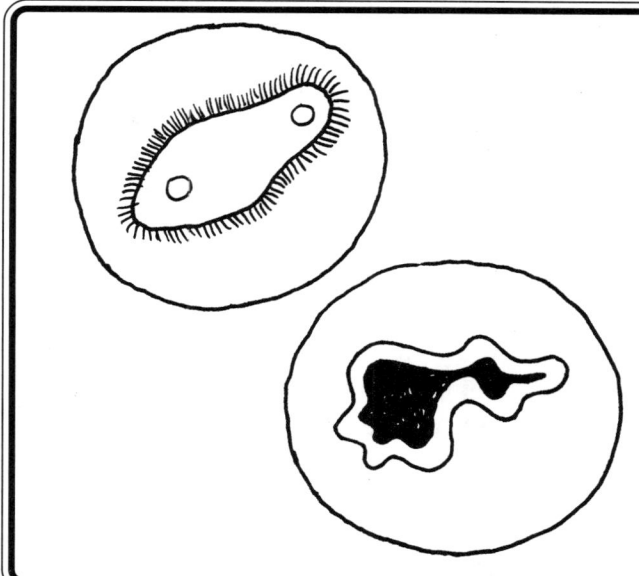

Microscopic Life

Look at some pond or creek water under a microscope. Do you see any single-celled animals? You can probably find a microscopic animal, such as a *paramecium* or an *amoeba,* if you look closely.

Draw in your journal how each animal looks under magnification. Label each of the pictures.

Write a paragraph describing the single-celled animal you find the most interesting. Give the creature a name and explain why you chose that name.

Microscopic Community

Read about single-celled animals. Pretend to be one. Which one are you? Why did you choose to be that microscopic animal?

Write a story about what it is like to live in your microscopic community. What do you eat? Where do you live, and are there any dangers there? Do you have any enemies to fear, and if so, who? If not, why not? What is the best thing about being a single-celled animal living in your microscopic community? Let your imagination run free when you write your story.

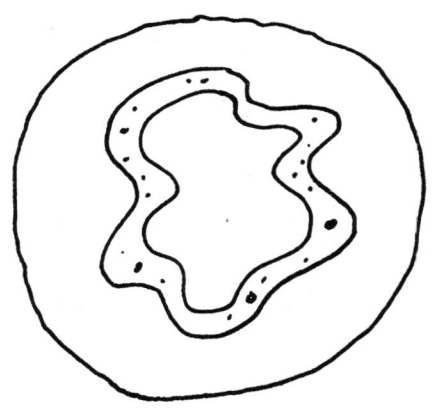

What Makes a Mammal a Mammal?

Why do some scientists group horses and cats together? Why are bats and birds not in the same group? Think of the reasons why animals may be grouped as they are.

Write a letter in your journal to a friend from another planet who has never seen an animal. In the letter, explain why the animals are sometimes grouped together. Include the animal groups of *mammals, reptiles, amphibians, birds, fish, insects,* and *spiders* in your letter. Use books from the library if you need help in explaining the categories.

© Carson-Dellosa Publ. CD-7317

What Am I?

In your journal, draw an animal which fits each description below. Write the animal classification for each picture. The classifications are listed in the lower left corner. Also, add an additional clue or two for each type under its picture.

1. We are warm-blooded.
   We have wings.
   We have two legs.
   We lay hard-shelled eggs.
   Feathers cover our bodies.

2. We are cold-blooded.
   We lay eggs.
   We have three body parts.
   We do not have backbones.
   We have exoskeletons.
   We have six legs.
   Many of us have wings.

3. We are cold-blooded.
   We have moist skin.
   We begin our lives in the water.
   When we become adults we grow legs and lungs.
   We breathe air but live near water.
   We lay jelly-coated eggs in water.

4. We are warm-blooded.
   We breathe air.
   Some of us live in water but most of us live on land.
   We bear live young and nurse our babies.
   Most of us have hair or fur on our bodies.

5. We are cold-blooded.
   Some of us are pets.
   We lay eggs or bear live young.
   We have scaly skin that has a slimy coating.
   We live and breathe under water.

6. We are cold-blooded.
   We have scales that are dry.
   We breathe air.
   Some of us live in water.
   Others live on land.
   We all lay our dry, leathery eggs on land.

7. We are cold-blooded.
   We lay eggs.
   We do not have backbones.
   We have two body parts and eight legs.
   Many of us spin webs.

- **mammals** • **fish**
- **spiders** • **birds**
- **reptiles** • **insects**
  • **amphibians**

Animal Life 20 © Carson-Dellosa Publ. CD-7317

Changing Stages of Life

Some animals look very different from their parents when they are born. They have to go through many changes before they become adults. This is called *metamorphosis*. Most insects undergo metamorphosis. Read about the two types—*complete* and *incomplete* metamorphosis. **List different insects for each group in your journal.**

Draw and label an insect that goes through a complete metamorphosis. Show each stage. Next, draw and label an insect that goes through an incomplete metamorphosis, again showing each stage. Compare the two insects, then write several paragraphs in your journal that contrast the two different types of changes.

The Life of a Monarch Butterfly

Read about the monarch butterfly. Pretend you are a monarch larva just emerging from your egg stage.

Write an autobiography in your journal that tells all about your life from the moment you emerge from an egg. Tell what you do at different life stages, such as the larva, pupa, or adult stage, and how you feel. Be creative. Tell about any exciting or frightening things that happen to you during your life. **Write about your plans for the future. Make a "photo" album by drawing a picture of yourself at each stage in your life.**

Vertebrates and Invertebrates

Think of how vertebrates and invertebrates are different. What limitations does a backbone give vertebrates? What limitations do invertebrates have because they lack a backbone? Imagine you—along with all other people—suddenly become invertebrates. You remain healthy and strong, but your life changes with the disappearance of your spine.

Write in your journal about how your life has changed. Describe how you move, how you look, how you eat, how you play, and so on. Tell whether you like the new you or not, and why.

Endothermic and Ectothermic

Find out whether you are an *endothermic* animal or an *ectothermic* one by referring to a science book or an encyclopedia. What other animals are like you?

In your journal, write as if you were teaching the class about the difference between these two types of animals. Be sure you explain the difference between the two. List the pros and cons of being an endothermic animal and being an ectothermic animal.

My Favorite Animal Group

What classification of animals intrigues you the most—mammal, reptile, bird, fish, insect, or amphibian? **In your journal, write your favorite animal classification and list all the animals in that class grouping that you can.** (Try to include at least six animals on your list.)

In your journal, write a paragraph or two that tells why you like this animal group the best, and include characteristics which make this group different from the other groups. Draw pictures of your two favorite animals in the group.

Animal Life

Diary of a Frog

Read about different frogs and decide which one you would like to be. You might like to be a poisonous one who lives in Africa, or you might rather be a bullfrog who lives in someone's backyard.

Pretend you are your chosen frog and compose a diary in your journal that follows your life. Begin at day one of your life, when you emerge from your egg. Write one entry for each different stage of life you experience. Date each entry as if you were really writing a diary.

Write about the changes that you undergo as you become an adult. How does it feel to grow legs, take your first breath of air, and undergo the other changes of a frog? **Write about any exciting things that happen in your life. Draw pictures to illustrate different special events in your diary.**

Human Animals

People are classified as animals in the world of science. **Explain how people are animals.** What characteristics do we share with all other animals, and which ones do we share only with other mammals? What makes us different from plants?

Write a few paragraphs in your journal about what makes humans different from all other animals.

Animal Adaptations: Camouflage

Some animals stand out from their environments, but some creatures blend in as much as possible. Some animals have natural camouflage to help them hide from other animals.

In your journal, write why you think an animal would want to blend in with its environment. List some animals that have natural camouflage. Circle the animals on your list that are prey for other animals.

List some animals that are predators who are also camouflaged. Write about why you think a predator needs to be able to hide.

© Carson-Dellosa Publ. CD-7317   23   *Animal Life*

Animal Life Supplementary Activities

Bird Feeders

This activity lets your class learn about the feeding preferences and habits of local birds. Begin by asking the students to observe what kinds of birds they see in the schoolyard. Have them read about the birds in a bird reference book, finding out what type of food each bird eats. An area store specializing in wild bird supplies could also be a valuable source for information. **Have the students record in their science journals the information gathered during their research.**

1. **Let the children design and build bird feeders for seed-eating birds.** They can use balsa wood, which is quite soft and easy to put together. They can also cut out shapes from cardboard that can then be smeared with peanut butter and sprinkled with different seeds. These simple bird feeders will still let the class observe which types of birds prefer specific types of seeds. The students can also make feeders out of empty cardboard and plastic milk cartons, plastic liter and larger soft drink bottles, and even egg cartons. Let the students use their imaginations and ingenuity to design and build feeders of all sorts and shapes.

2. **Purchase different seeds, including basic birdseed mix, sunflower seeds, shelled peanuts, and, if possible, specialty seeds such as fennel and thistle.** Also have peanut butter and bread on hand. Let the class decide which type of feeder would be most desirable to a specific bird species; then let them choose which type of seed would be preferred by that bird. Have children fill the feeders or attach the seeds on bread with peanut butter. Hang different feeders outside within view of the classroom. This way the class can observe the feeders and visiting birds throughout the day. If the feeders cannot be seen from the classroom, you will need to schedule time for the class to visit the feeders twice a day.

3. **If the feeders are within view of the classroom, have the class keep a chart that reflects the number of birds, the types of birds, and the frequency of visits by each type of bird.** If the class is unable to observe the feeders from your room, have them measure and record the amount of food eaten by the birds each time the class visits the feeders. To do this, simply have the class record the starting amount of food, then measure again and subtract this amount each time they visit a feeder.

4. **The class may find other animals—such as squirrels, chipmunks, and other rodents—at the feeders.** See if they can devise a way to keep the non-bird visitors from the bird feeders. For instance, the students may try feeding the small mammals a different food at a different location to keep them from the birdseed.

5. **Have the class draw some conclusions from the things they have observed.** How might they improve the design of the feeder? What types of bird food did each bird species like most? Did the type of feeder affect what kinds of birds visited the feeder?

"Eggs"- Ray Vision

Some animals, such as birds, fish, and reptiles, lay eggs instead of giving birth to live offspring. Eggshells protect the baby animals inside and the eggs contain nutrients the animals need to develop. **The following exercise will allow the students to look inside an egg and identify the yolk without cracking the egg!**

Materials needed for one "eggs"-ray box:
- shoe box
- egg (preferably a white jumbo-sized egg)
- small flashlight (shorter than height of shoe box)
- black tempera paint *or* black spray paint
- large paint brush (for use with tempera paint)
- crayons and markers
- scissors
- masking tape

Directions:
1. Outdoors or in a well-ventilated room, have the students paint the inside of the shoe box black, including the inside of the lid. If using spray paint, have an adult help students. Allow the box and lid to dry completely.
2. Let the children decorate the outside of the box to resemble a nest.
3. Have the children use scissors to cut a hole about 1½" in diameter out of the center of one of the shoe box ends. You should be able to cradle the egg in the hole without it falling through.
4. Turn on the flashlight. Place it in the box with the light facing up. Use masking tape to hold the flashlight in position.
5. Put the lid on the box. The light should shine up through the hole. Let each child cradle an egg in the hole.
6. The light should illuminate the inside of the egg. **Ask the students to write down their observations and draw diagrams of what they see in their science journals.**

"Eggs"-amine a Fertilized Egg

1. **Assign a small group of students to research how to incubate and care for fertilized eggs.** Have them present their research to the class. Obtain fertilized chicken eggs from a farm. Make arrangements to return the chicks to the farm once they have hatched or find someone who is willing to care for them in the proper setting. Ask the class to pick a method by which to incubate the eggs and do whatever is needed so that the eggs may hatch.

2. **Assign another small group of students to research the stages through which a chick develops.** Have them draw a chart or create a bulletin board explaining the different stages. As the hatching date gets closer, use the "eggs"-ray box (above) to see the baby chick inside the egg. The teacher should assist the students with the experiment since the egg must be handled *very* carefully.

3. **Ask the students to predict what day the egg will hatch.** Make a poster with the students' names and their predictions. Offer a special reward, such as an egg-shaped piece of candy, to the student who picks the correct date. If no one picks the correct date, give the reward to the student who gave the closest prediction. Reward all students with a treat for participating.

Ecosystems

The Activity Boxes in this section can enhance your students' understanding of the differences and similarities between plants and animals. They will explore how plants and animals are dependent on one another and how they are both important parts of ecosystems or habitats.

Natural Symmetry

What is symmetry? Find out what it is by looking up the word in a dictionary or science book. Also research the meanings of *bilateral symmetry* and *radial symmetry*. Explore nature to find samples of the different types of symmetry. **Trace or draw what you find in your journal. Draw lines to divide the pictures to show how they are symmetrical.** Label the types of symmetry each one represents. For instance, if you found a starfish, you would trace it, draw lines to show its *radial symmetry*, and label it "radial symmetry." Likewise, you would trace or draw a dogwood leaf, draw a line to show its *bilateral symmetry*, and label it "bilateral symmetry." Try to list at least five objects that are symmetrical.

Are you symmetrical, and if so, how? **In your journal, draw an outline of yourself and divide the outline of your body as you did the nature objects. Label the outline with the type of symmetry it represents.**

Living Cells teacher directions—For the Living Cells activity below, the students will need a few microscopes, flat toothpicks, clean slides, cover slips, pieces of elodea (a water plant available at most aquarium-supply stores), and onion skins. Tell each student to prepare his first slide by putting a drop of clean water on it. Have him very gently scrape the inside of his cheek with the flat end of a toothpick. Tell him to spread out the collected skin cells in the water drop and to discard the used toothpick. The students will not be able to see the cells on the toothpick. The cells can only be seen under a microscope because they are so small. Instruct the students to put cover slips over the skin samples and to examine the cells under the microscope.

Have students look at the onion and elodea cells under the microscope. Be sure they use only a thin piece of skin from an inner layer of the onion and a thin piece of elodea.

Living Cells

The smallest unit of life is a cell. Everything that is alive is made of one or more cells. With your teacher's help, look at your own skin cells under a microscope.

In your journal, draw how the cells look. Next, look at the cells of a onion skin under magnification. Then, look at some plant cells. **Draw both the onion and plant cells.**

Write a paragraph that compares your skin cells with the onion and plant cells. How are they similar? How are they different?

ECOSYSTEMS

Plants and Animals

How are animals dependent on plants? What would happen to the animals if suddenly there were no plants? People are animals, too. What would happen to you if plants suddenly disappeared?

Write an imaginary story in your journal describing what might cause all the plants to disappear and how the animals would be affected. Tell how life on earth would change, including your own life. What would you eat? How would our air be affected? Where would animals live, and where would you live?

My Place in the Food Web

Think about all the foods you ate over the past two days and list as many of them as you can recall in your journal. If a food item has many ingredients, list as many of them as you can. For cookies, you would list butter, eggs, flour, sugar, and whatever other ingredients make the cookies, like chocolate chips or peanut butter, for example.

Find out what a *food web* is by looking up the term in a science book. **Make a food web in your journal that shows all of the foods in your diet from the past two days.** Show the source where each of these items gets food, too, and include that information in your web. A field of wheat gets energy from the sun and nutrients from the soil, for instance, and a cow gets its food from grasses and grains.

Write an explanation of how your food web works. Name the lowest plants or animals in the web. (These are the plants and animals that do not rely on other plants or animals for survival.)

© Carson-Dellosa Publ. CD-7317

Ecosystems

Plants, Animals, and Food

Diagram a food web in your journal for a habitat that interests you. Show which plants are eaten by animals, and which animals are eaten by other animals. What would happen if a link in the food web was removed? What if more links were removed? How would it affect the whole habitat? **In your journal, write what you think would happen.**

Pollution and Food

Think about how pollution affects the environment. Fish and other animals eat or drink pollution that is in water. When we eat polluted foods, the pollution gets inside us. **In your journal, list different kinds of pollution and how they could harm the food web. List possible sources of these pollutants.**

Write a letter to your state senator, your congressional representative, or the Environmental Protection Agency asking for help in controlling pollution. For example, perhaps more safeguards could be placed on oil barges to reduce the number of ocean oil spills. In your letter, tell how the pollution can harm the environment, and how it can get into the food we and other animals eat. Suggest a way to get people to protect the environment. **Keep a copy of the letter in your journal.**

Ecosystems

Think of an ecosystem that interests you. What makes it a system? How do the plants and animals interact to make the system work?

In your journal, write an explanation of what an ecosystem is. Tell what makes up an ecosystem. Use the ecosystem which interests you as an example and explain how this ecosystem is different from another one. How are all ecosystems alike?

Ecosystems © Carson-Dellosa Publ. CD-7317

An Ecosystem Speaks

What do you have an interest in learning more about—a forest, jungle, sea, or pond? Pretend you are that ecosystem, including all the animals, plants, and land. You have a voice that people can hear and understand for one day.

In your journal, write what you would say to people. Tell the people if they are harming you and how, what they can do to help you be strong and healthy, and any warnings or pleas you have. Tell how you and people can better coexist. Remember, you can be heard for only one day, so be sure you are organized and clear as you write your speech.

Alien Visitor from Zart

A visitor from the planet Zart just landed, and you are the alien's tour guide. Think about what natural areas you want to show the alien. You can take the visitor any place on Earth, but you have time to show him only one place.

Write a story in your journal that tells where you took the alien, why you chose that location, and the alien's response. Tell about the ecosystem you visited—where on earth it is found, what makes it special, what climate it has, what plants and animals live there, and so on. Draw a picture of yourself and the alien in the place you visited.

A 12-Inch Hike

Go outside and choose a place to go on a "12-inch hike." Take a ruler, a magnifying glass, and a piece of string or yarn with you. Use your ruler to measure out a 12-inch square of land, and use the string to mark it off. Examine your plot of land carefully with your magnifying glass.

In your journal, draw what you see living in your marked-off plot—both plants and animals. List the animals that you see on the land. List the sounds you hear and the odors you smell in and around your plot of land.

Pretend you are a travel agent who is selling 12-inch hikes on your plot of land. **In your journal, write a sales pitch about the hike, what you find there, and so on.** The buyers of the trip can be anyone or anything: humans, ants, butterflies—whatever you want. Try to make the hike sound like the best trip in the world!

Ecosystems Supplementary Activities

Science Under the Sea (or Science in the Forest, etc.)

To begin this activity, explain to the students that the ocean itself (or the forest, the Arctic, even a suburban area!) can be considered a large ecosystem, with different types of animals and plants living together.

1. **Ask the students to find pictures in magazines or newspapers (or draw pictures) of plants and animals that live in the sea or in the chosen ecosystem.** Have the students arrange the pictures on a bulletin board and make a label for the ecosystem being studied.
2. **Tell the students to research the plants and animals in the pictures and record the information in their journals.** Are they endangered or threatened? What do the animals eat? Are the plants a food source for any animals? Do the animals and/or plants have any unique features or characteristics?
3. **Have the students create a "fact card" for each plant or animal on an index card.** Be sure to have students include the name of the plant or animal, any special characteristics, and any other interesting facts they can find.
4. **Read the fact cards aloud to the class and ask them to match the cards with the corresponding pictures on the bulletin board.** Complete the bulletin board by attaching the fact cards.

Learning About Pollution's Effects

Often, it is difficult for students to understand the actual impact of their actions on the environment. In grades 4 through 6, children usually learn about natural resource management, but they can still be unaware of its practical applications. These simple activities can help students understand the impact of their actions on the environment.

1. **Let the students see how water pollution affects the food chain.** Divide the class into two groups. Provide each group of students with two jars that have about an inch of water in the bottom of each jar. Instruct the students to add a few drops of food coloring, in a color of their choice, to each jar. Give each group of students a white flower (such as Queen Anne's Lace, carnation, or daisy) and a stalk of celery with a freshly-cut end. Have the students cut the flower stem at an angle to help the flower take in water, and then let them put the flower in one jar. Have the students stand the celery, cut end down, in the second jar. After a few hours, or the next day, ask the class what has happened to the flowers and celery. **Have the students record the results in their science journals.** You might need to cut the celery again and look at the veins inside it to see that it has become dyed by the colored water. Link these activities to pollution through a class discussion about how plants take in pollution. **Have the students write a few paragraphs in their science journals on what they have learned.**

2. **Ask the class to explain how water pollution affects the whole food web, such as when animals consume plants that have absorbed polluted water.** Ask the students to discuss ways to reduce water pollution, such as using environmentally-safe detergents and soaps, limiting the use of pesticides and herbicides, and being conscientious with other toxic items. **Have students research where to dispose of toxic substances, such as motor oil, paint, and insecticides, in their area and list these disposal locations in their journals.**

3. **Another way to promote concern for the environment is to have the class go on a litter hunt.** After cautioning the students about the potential health hazards of some litter, provide them with disposable rubber gloves and garbage bags to collect all the litter they can find in a selected area. Have them sort the litter by material and recycle whatever they can in your area. Ask them why people litter, and how the class can influence people to stop. Ask how the litter affects the environment. **Ask students to list in their journals as many ways as they can that recycling helps the environment. Have them draw *before* and *after* pictures of the area where they conducted their hunt, and then let them make posters to educate the school about littering and its effects on the environment.**

Protecting Wildlife

The following activities can teach the students about the specific endangered species in their area and show them some steps they can take to help protect these vulnerable animals. Children can use their science journals to record information about this subject.

1. **Ask the students to find out what species are endangered or threatened in your area or state.** Have them pick one animal from this list and find out what is threatening it—habitat destruction, pollution, or lack of food, for instance. They should find out what is causing the problem. Is the habitat being destroyed as people build more homes, offices, malls, and so on? Is it being destroyed because of mining or some other industry's possible harmful use of the land? Is it because of some other threat?

2. **Tell the students to read all they can about the endangered animal.** Have students find out where else the animal is (or used to be) found. How long has the animal been endangered or threatened? How quickly has its population declined, and is it still on the decline or has it started to come back? Have students find out about organizations dedicated to saving the animal and what sort of programs or procedures the organizations are using. If possible, invite someone involved in saving the animal to visit your class, or have the students write to the organization for information. Try to set up a field trip to learn more about the endangered animal and the programs trying to protect it.

3. **Have the students write to their state representatives and senators to encourage them to help protect the endangered animal.** Also, have students make posters to help educate other students in the school.

4. **Encourage the class to hold a fund-raiser to earn money to give to the organizations working to help protect the endangered animal.** The class may hold a car wash, bake sale, special performance, raffle with a prize the class makes, recycling drive, or some other event to raise money.

5. **Invite the class to write reports or create a skit about the endangered animal and how people can help to protect it.** See if they can present their skit or reports on a local news show or some other community program.

6. **Have the class list other endangered animals in the world and find out what has caused their decline.** Encourage them to list in their journals ways to prevent the further decline of plants and animals in the world. Teach them about the hazards of litter. The plastic rings that hold six-packs of soft drinks, for instance, can kill animals that get tangled in the rings. A solution is to cut up the rings before discarding them so animals will not get snagged in them.

Ecosystems

Matter, Energy, and Light

This set of Activity Boxes can enhance your class's studies of matter and different forms of energy.

What Is Matter?

Research the different properties of *matter*. Water vapor and other gases are sometimes invisible, but they have weight. They are considered matter, too. **In your science journal, list the three forms of matter and write your thoughts about each of the different forms. Write an amusing poem describing an aspect of matter that intrigues you.**

Energy Cowboy

Imagine that the world has just run out of natural gas, coal, oil, and nuclear energy. You are an *energy cowboy* who can *rope* the sun, water, and wind. **In your journal, write a story that tells how you harness solar energy, the wind, and running water.** The nature you capture heats homes and water when needed, cools buildings when needed, makes light bulbs and other electrical appliances work, and powers motor vehicles. In your story, explain how you harness nature. Use your imagination as well as your knowledge of energy and how it can be changed from one form into another.

Power Plants

What happens when you turn on a light switch? What is the source of the electricity? Find out about your town's power plant. How does it generate electricity? Some power plants use steam, others burn fuel such as coal or natural gas, and others use nuclear energy. Find out how your power plant takes one form of energy and makes electrical energy.

In your journal, explain in your own words the process of producing and transporting electricity. Illustrate the procedure with diagrams.

Transferring Heat teacher directions—For the heat transfer experiments below, encourage younger students to use the sun as a heat source. They could heat a piece of dark paper in the sun, and then observe the reaction of an ice cube laid on it, for instance. Another experiment could show how the sun heats up a cup of water. The starting temperature of the water should be recorded. After the cup sits in a sunny spot for an hour, the ending temperature should then be recorded and compared with the beginning temperature.

Transferring Heat

Heat is a form of energy. Energy can be transferred from one substance to another.

Create an experiment that shows how heat energy can be taken from one object and given to another. **Using the scientific method, write an experiment in your journal, stating how heat might be transferred from one object to another.** Describe the materials you will use. Record the steps of your experiment in detail so that someone else could follow them and reach the same conclusion.

Conduct the experiment, recording your observations, and stating your conclusion on a separate page. Ask a classmate to follow the steps of your experiment and compare his or her results with yours.

Making and Retaining Heat teacher directions—You will need to supply the students with a piece of standard bubble wrap, water, cups, white paper, black paper, tape, and a thermometer to conduct the experiment. Do this activity as a class demonstration, then let the children take turns recording the water temperatures.

Making and Retaining Heat

Put three cups containing the same amount of water on a sunny windowsill. Record their starting temperatures (they should start at the same temperature). Wrap white paper around one cup, black paper around another, and bubble wrap around the third one. Record the water temperatures after twenty minutes, forty minutes, and after an hour. **In your journal, make a chart of how the temperatures compare.**

Using the information you learned from the experiment above, think about how your home retains heat when the weather is cold outside. How do you and other animals keep warm when the weather is cold? **In your journal, list the sources of heat for those situations.** Imagine what would happen if there were no shelters, insulation, stoves, or heaters. How could you keep warm on a cold day? How might you heat things to eat and drink? How might you warm the room? **Write in your journal about ways you could make heat to keep warm.**

Matter, Energy, and Light

Releasing the Sun's Energy teacher directions—For the Releasing the Sun's Energy activity below, a simple compost pile (consisting of yard waste) is required. See if your school's grounds crew will pile all the grass, hedge trimmings, and other yard waste in one place. Keep the pile damp. The layers near the middle and bottom of the pile will begin to decompose, and they will release heat. Your students can feel this by using a rake to turn the pile and then holding their hands over the upturned layers.

Releasing the Sun's Energy

When plants undergo photosynthesis, they trap the sun's energy inside them. When the plants die, they release the energy. Use a book from the library to find out how to make a compost pile. Make a compost pile either at school or at home following your teacher's directions. If you do this experiment at school, your teacher will ask the principal for permission to create a compost pile. If you do this experiment at home, make sure you ask your parents for permission. **Predict what form the plant's energy takes when it is released, and record your hypothesis in your journal.**

Use a rake to turn the compost pile. Observe whether your hypothesis was correct or not. **Write a few paragraphs in your journal explaining how the sun's energy is contained and released in a compost pile.**

Solar Energy and Life

Pretend that the sun suddenly burned out! Life on earth is in danger because green plants, which require sunlight to undergo photosynthesis, are an essential link in the food web. Without the sun's light, these plants have no way to make their food. People and many animals rely on plants as nourishment.

Do you think people can think of a way to save all life? **Write a story in your journal that describes a solution to this problem.** Use your knowledge of light, changing one form of energy into another, and the food web as you write your story.

Electrical Currents teacher directions—For the Electrical Currents activity below, you can purchase the materials to build the switches at an electronic supply or hardware store. For each switch, the students will need a D-size battery, a 1.5-volt bulb in a bulb holder, a large rubber band, two steel thumbtacks, a small piece of cardboard, a steel paper clip, and three copper wires whose ends are stripped. Follow these steps to make the switch:

Step 1 Have the students touch one end of a wire to the indented end of the battery, secure the wire in place with the rubber band, and then attach the other end of the wire to the terminal on the bulb holder.

Step 2 Tell the students to touch one end of a second wire to the knob on the end of the battery and secure it in place with the same rubber band, and then attach the other end of the wire to a thumbtack stuck in the cardboard.

Step 3 Instruct the students to then attach the third wire to the other bulb terminal and to the other tack, stuck in the cardboard about an inch from the first tack.

Step 4 Have the students loop one end of the paper clip around one tack and bend the clip up so it rests just above, not on, the second tack. To complete the circuit, students should press the "switch" (push the clip against the second tack).

Electrical Currents

Electricity has to travel in a path to reach its destination. We use wires to direct its path. Make a simple switch with the materials and directions your teacher provides to see how electricity moves in a path.

Make a diagram of your switch in your journal. Be sure each item in your diagram is clearly labeled, so a friend following the diagram could make a complete circuit.

Look up the terms *insulator* and *conductor* in a science book or encyclopedia. **Write the two definitions in your journal. Explain in your journal why insulators are just as important as conductors (think of a copper wire enclosed in plastic). How do the terms relate to the switch you just made?**

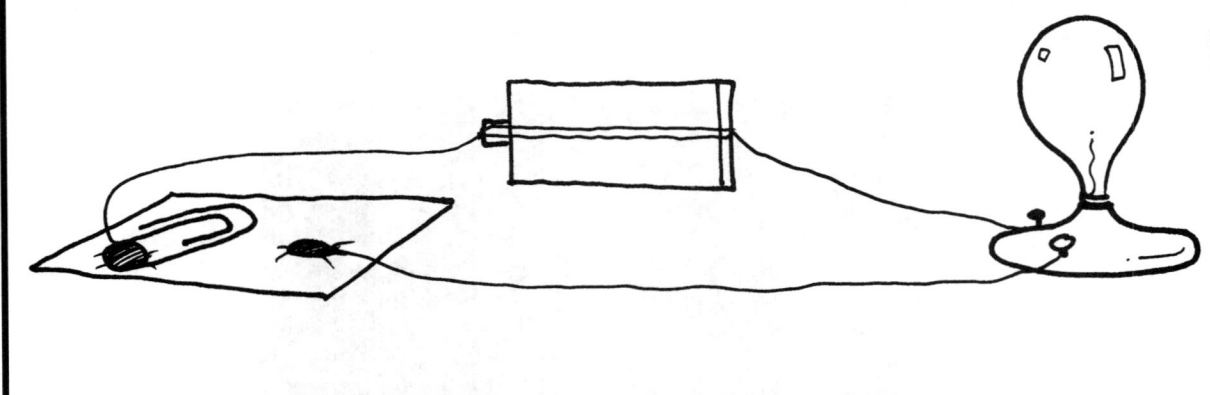

Matter, Energy, and Light

Conserving Energy to Save the Planet

When we use an electrical appliance, such as a lamp, a number of things take place to make it produce light. Electrical energy is turned into light energy. The electrical energy comes from a power plant. The power plant uses another form of energy to make electricity. It may use coal, oil, or natural gas. When we use a motor vehicle, we use gas and oil. We have to take from the environment to use these things.

Think about how you can help save the planet by conserving energy. **In your journal, list at least five ways you and your classmates could conserve energy.**

Pretend you are a presidential candidate concerned with energy conservation. In your journal, write a speech to get people to vote for you by explaining your plan to conserve energy and help save the planet.

Sound Energy

Sound is a form of energy. It comes from vibrating objects. Research sound energy in a science book or encyclopedia. **In your journal, write a descriptive paragraph that explains how vibrations create sounds that we hear. Draw and label the parts of the ear to help make the explanation clear.**

Sound Walk

Walk outside for ten or fifteen minutes, then in your journal list the sounds you hear and what you think the source for each sound is. Draw a picture of what the different sounds make you think of or how the sounds make you feel—not a picture of the source of the sound.

Back in the classroom, **write a few paragraphs that tell what the experience was like for you.** If you enjoyed it, why? If you didn't like it, why not?

Communication System for the Hearing-Impaired

Braille is a system of writing for people who cannot see. It uses a series of raised bumps that the blind read with their fingers. Think of how you could make a communications system for people who cannot hear. Pretend this system would help them to "hear" the radio, television, stereo, or voices over the telephone.

Use vibrations that can be felt as the foundation for your system. The speed or frequency of a vibrating object could stand for different letters or words, or maybe a system of starting and stopping vibrations would work. Use your imagination. **In your journal, explain your system in a proposal to the U.S. Patent Office. Name the device and include illustrations, diagrams, and quotations from imaginary people who have used it.**

Sun Clocks teacher directions—To make the sundials in the Sun Clocks activity below, each student will need a large, sturdy paper plate, some modelling clay, and an unsharpened pencil. Instruct each class member to put a small mound of clay in the middle of the plate and to stick the pencil in the clay at an angle. The pencil will act as a pointer. Tell the students to place their sundials in a sunny, open area outdoors, making sure the pointers tilt to the north. Check the direction with a compass. (The pointer in a true sundial would be angled perfectly according to the latitude of the city in which the sundial rests. For the purposes of this exercise, however, it is sufficient to angle the pointer toward the north.) On every hour, have each student mark where his pencil's shadow falls on the plate and to label the mark with the current hour.

Enrich the sundial activity by connecting it with math. Remind the class that the earth rotates one complete revolution (360 degrees) every twenty-four hours. Explain that scientists have determined that the earth moves fifteen degrees every hour (15 degrees x 24 hours = 360 degrees). This information will enable your students to measure the accuracy of the marks on their sundials. Have them use protractors to measure the angles between hour marks on their sundials. Each angle should be fifteen degrees, or very close to that.

Sun Clocks

Long ago, people did not have clocks to tell time. They had to use the sun. They made sun clocks, called *sundials* or *shadow clocks*, to help them keep track of time.

Read about different sundials and draw a picture of one or two in your journal, then create a sundial or shadow clock of your own following your teacher's instructions. List the materials you will use, write the steps to set up the clock, and explain how to use it in your journal, too.

Test your clock to see how accurate it is. Why will your sundial not work at night? When else or where else would it not work?

Abracadabra—New Colors!

You are a scientist on a planet that has only these three colors: red, yellow, and blue. Everyone is tired of these colors, and the people have asked you to work your science magic to create some new colors.

Set up your laboratory (desk) with these items: eye droppers; toothpicks; white paper; and red, yellow, and blue paints. What new colors do you think you can create? **In your journal, write your hypothesis and an outline of your experiment.** Be creative but use what you know about the primary colors. Write color equations such as Y + B = G (Yellow + Blue = Green) to explain your experiments. Test your hypothesis by mixing the colors together on the white paper. Was your hypothesis correct? **Record your results in your journal.** Try several different color combinations.

Matter, Energy, and Light

Favorite Color Survey

Survey at least thirty people to find out what their favorite colors are. Have them tell you why they like their favorite colors. (**Be sure you take notes in your journal so you will remember what they say.**)

In your journal, make a graph that shows the results of your survey. Summarize the results of your survey including different reasons why people like each color. Write what your favorite color is, why, and where it fits into the graph.

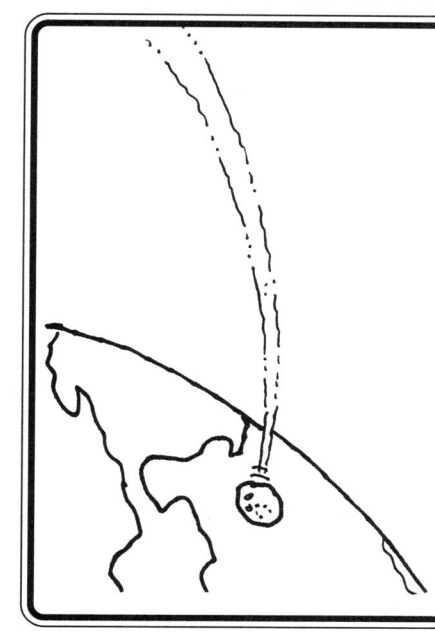

Putting Colors in Their Places

A giant meteor has crashed into the earth, and the jolt from its impact has mixed up the colors in nature. The leaves on trees and the grass, once green, are now orange. The ocean, once blue-green, is now purple. The blue sky has turned green, orange pumpkins are red, and red tomatoes are purple. Purple plums are black, and oranges have turned red.

It's up to you to fix things. Sometimes you will have to take away colors from objects. Other times you will need to add colors to them. **Write in your journal about the way you straighten out the mess.** Include all the things mentioned in the first paragraph and anything else that is mixed up that you think you might find. Write equations, such as G - Y = B (Green - Yellow = Blue), that show how you add or remove colors to return each object to its original color.

Rainbow of Colors teacher directions—Explain to your students that white light is made of seven different light waves, each with its own wavelength and color (red, orange, yellow, green, blue, indigo, and violet). When light enters water, the water acts as a prism, making the different waves separate from each other. In the following activity, light is refracted and bounced onto a blank wall, where a color spectrum will appear. (Your class can also cast a rainbow on the wall by catching the sunlight in a hand-held prism.)

Rainbow of Colors

There is a spectrum of color inside every sunbeam. Do you know which colors appear, and in what order, when light is refracted? Find out by making a prism and directing sunlight through it or by shining a bright light on it. You will need some water, a glass baking pan, and a mirror. Work in a very sunny spot in front of a wall. Fill the pan with water. Stand the mirror in the pan so it leans against the side of the pan as shown. Slowly move the mirror back and forth to catch the sunlight on it. Look at the wall where the mirror reflects the light.

What colors did you find? **In your journal, list the colors in the order in which you saw them. Explain in your journal how you used the water to expose the sunlight's colors. Color a picture of the rainbow in your journal.**

© Carson-Dellosa Publ. CD-7317

Matter, Energy, and Light

Spectrum Spinners teacher directions—For the Spectrum Spinners activity below, you will need to provide the class with unlined index cards, scissors, short sharpened pencils, and markers or crayons. When the colored discs are assembled and then spun, the students will see how the colors combine to make white.

Spectrum Spinners

Write in your journal the names of the seven colors that make up white light. To see how the colors blend to make white, cut out a circle from a white, unlined index card or tagboard, using the pattern shown. Poke a sharp pencil through the center. Remove the pencil. Color each wedge a color of the rainbow. Be sure the colors are in the right order. Put the pencil back in the hole, and spin the circle like a top. What happens to the colors? **Jot down the equation for making white light in your journal, then write a note to a friend explaining what happened.**

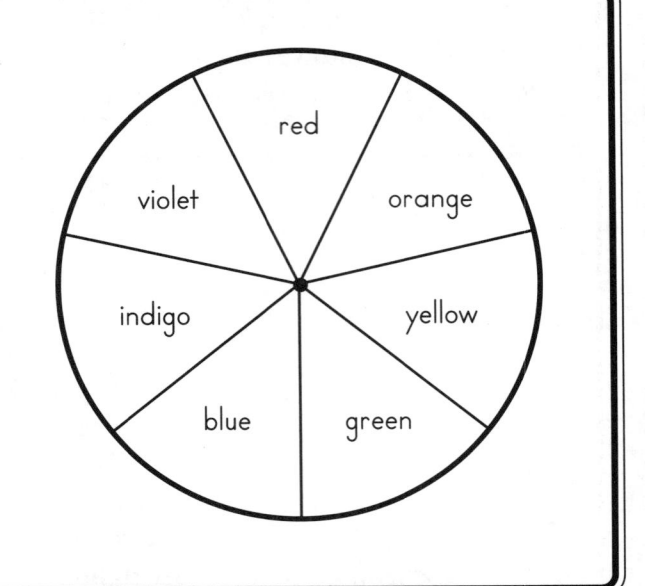

Spin-Off Colors

Make other spinners like your spectrum spinner, only this time do not use all seven colors. Try different color combinations. Sometimes, use two colors; other times, use three or four colors. **Record the colors you use on diagrams in your journal. Before you spin the spinners, record the colors you predict you will see on the spinning discs. Next to your predictions, write the actual colors you see.**

Colorful Poetry

List the colors of the color spectrum in the order that they appear in a rainbow. **In your journal, write a poem that describes all of the colors.** Be sure you mention the colors in the order that they appear, beginning either with red or with violet. Color pictures to illustrate your poem. Pick your favorite of the seven colors. **Write another poem that is all about that color.** You can mention other colors in this poem, but only if you are showing how your favorite color is different from any others.

Matter, Energy, and Light

Visiting Planet MB-11

You have just landed on the imaginary planet MB-11, in the Dog galaxy. When you exit your spacecraft and take your first look around MB-11, you realize there are no colors here. Everything is in shades of gray, as if you were watching a black-and-white television show. Some friendly aliens come to greet you, and you ask them to show you around the planet.

Pick up the story from here and write the rest of it in your journal. Explain to your new friends what colors are. Describe the seven colors of the spectrum and the shades within them. Since the people on MB-11 have never before seen or heard of colors, you have to relate colors to things such as emotions, sensations, and so on. Try to find a way to create colors for your new friends on Planet MB-11, or take them with you for a short visit to Earth.

The Science in Sunsets teacher directions—For the Science in Sunsets activity below, provide a flashlight, one tablespoon milk (or about one-half to one teaspoon of powdered milk or creamer), and a glass of water. When the students have completed the activity, explain to them that the color of the water appeared bluish when the light was shown from above because the light was less scattered, so the shorter, blue light waves were reflected. The color turned a reddish-orange when the light came from the side because the light waves were more scattered, and only the longer red and orange waves got through the liquid. This is similar to what happens to light in the atmosphere at sunrise and sunset. At these times, the sun is low on the horizon and the sun's rays must pass through more atmosphere, including more particles of dust, smoke, and pollution, which stop the shorter wavelengths.

The Science in Sunsets

There is a reason the sky appears in shades of red and yellow during sunrise and sunset, just as there is a reason the sky looks blue during the day. This experiment will help you understand the science in sunsets and other sky colors. All you need is a clear glass of water, some milk, a flashlight, and a clear spot on a wall.

Put about 1 tablespoon of milk in the water; it should look cloudy without stirring. Shine the flashlight from above the glass and onto the milky water. What color does the water become? Now shine the flashlight from the side of the glass, so that it goes through the glass and onto the wall. What color is the water now? **Write a summary in your journal that explains why you think the milky water takes on a bluish cast when the light comes from above and a reddish-orange color when the light comes from the side of the glass.**

Why the Sky Has Colors

If you have ever seen a sunrise, you know that the sky turns many shades of reddish-orange and yellow as the sun rises from the horizon. During a clear day, the sky looks blue. It turns shades of red, pink, orange, and yellow again during sunset.

Write a folk tale in your journal that explains why the sky is blue, why sunrises and sunsets are in shades of reddish-orange, or why the sky has colors.

Seeing Light and Color

Your eyes can see light and color. Part of the eye has cells that let you see colors; other cells in the eye let you see light. Find out the name of each type of cell. In your journal, draw a diagram of your eye, and include the cells that let you see light and the ones that let you see color. **Write a paragraph to explain how the eye works.**

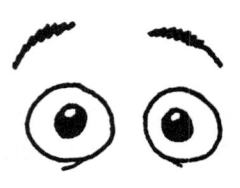

Eye Tricks

In your journal, define what you think an *optical illusion* is. Look at each set of illustrations below. Predict which line, A or B, you think is longer, and which circle is larger, 1 or 2; then use rulers to check your predictions. Circle the optical illusions that tricked your eye. **Write in your journal about the tricks your eyes played on you and why you think that happened.** Read about optical illusions in a resource book and then see if your explanation was correct about why these "tricks" occur. **Record the results of the activity in your journal. Were your predictions correct?**

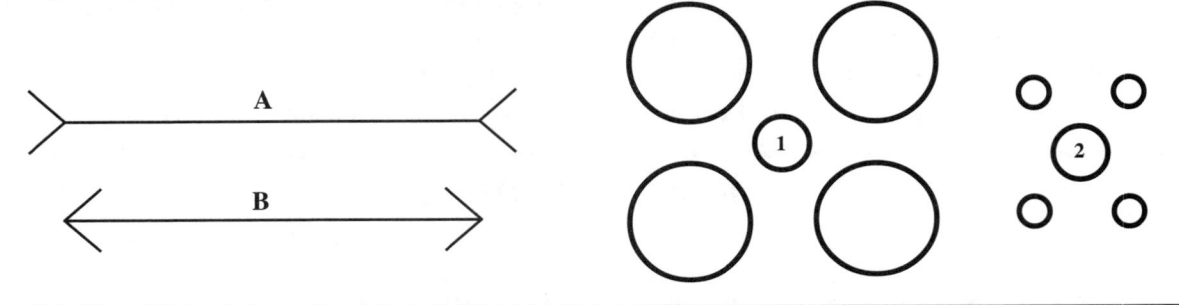

Visual Perceptions teacher directions—You will need to provide index cards, a stapler, pencils, and crayons for the students to perform the Visual Perceptions activity below. When students roll the pencils in their hands, the fish will appear to be in the fish bowl.

Visual Perceptions

Fold an index card in half. Draw and color a fish bowl on one side and a fish on the other side. Make sure the fold of the index card is at the top of the pictures. Staple the cards closely to each side of the pencil with the fold side up. Watch the pictures as you hold the pencil between flat palms and roll it quickly, causing the card to flip around very fast. What appears to happen to the fish? **In your journal, write a paragraph about the visual experiment and what you think causes this to happen.**

Matter, Energy, and Light

Matter, Energy, and Light
Supplementary Activities

Sound Dictionary

Assign one sound term or topic to a small group of students, allow them time to do research, and then ask them to write a report on their findings to share with the rest of the class. Some terms or topics to include are *frequency*, *resonance*, *pitch*, *wavelength*, *sonic boom*, *the Doppler Effect*, *sonar/echolocation*, and *ultrasonic*. Have each group of students tell what their term means and why it is important to the study of sound. Compile the reports into a notebook and label it "Sound Dictionary."

Sound Mysteries

Become a sound sleuth! Once the class has compiled their sound dictionary, ask them to investigate some of the sound mysteries below, or you may wish to add your own sound mysteries for them to solve. The following activities will allow the students to explore sound and its scientific characteristics on their own or in small groups. Once they have solved the mysteries, ask students to share their discoveries with the rest of the class.

- Ludwig van Beethoven was a famous German musical composer, yet some of his greatest works (including his Symphony no. 5) were written *after* he began to lose his hearing. How might he have been able to do this? Given what they have learned about the nature of sound, ask the students to write down a possible explanation. You may also want to have the students do research on Beethoven to see how he dealt with this disability and continued to create wonderful music.

- An avalanche is a large amount of loosened snow, earth, and rock which slides down a mountain. Avalanches can be very destructive, and are sometimes caused by sound. Ask the students to investigate how sound can cause an avalanche to happen.

- When you hold a large seashell to your ear, you can often hear a roaring noise like that of the sea. Some people say that you are hearing an echo of the sea inside the shell. What do the students think? Ask the students to do research to discover why a roaring sound is heard when the shell is placed next to the ear and what the sound really is.

- Bats are nocturnal animals, which means they usually only come out at night. Bats have poor eyesight, yet they are able to use sound to "see" obstacles to avoid when they are flying as well as to find insects to eat. Ask the students to explain how a bat uses sound to avoid danger and to find food.

The Solar System, Weather, and Rocks and Minerals

The Activity Boxes in this section can enhance your lesson plans on Earth studies, and help your students gain a deeper understanding of and appreciation for the Earth, its climate changes and seasons, and the rocks and minerals of which it is made.

Our Star, the Sun

The planets in our solar system orbit a star. We call this star the sun. How does its size compare to other stars in our galaxy? Is it the largest star in our galaxy? If not, what is the largest? **In your journal, write down your answers and then check resource books about the sun and other stars to see if you were accurate.**

Write a poem about the sun. Try to mention any unique features of the sun, such as sun spots, in your poem. Draw a picture of the sun to illustrate your poem.

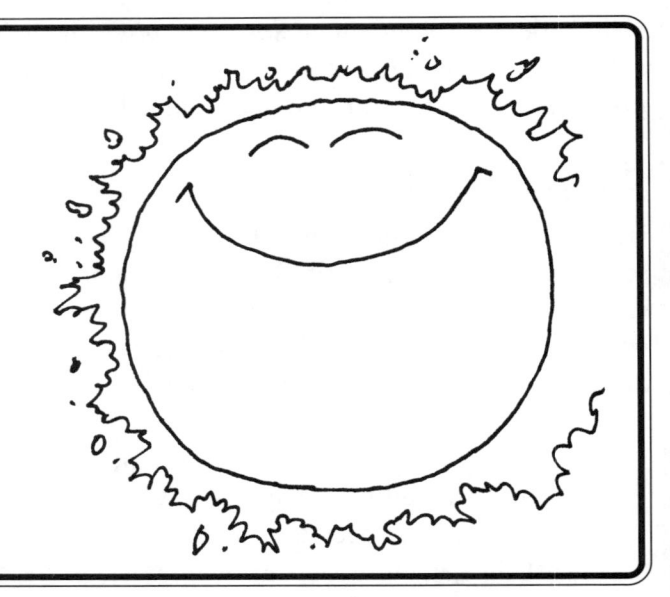

Our Solar System teacher directions—For the solar system activity below, use the following list of planetary representations to demonstrate how the planets compare to each other in size: Sun—circle cut from yellow paper, 30 inches in diameter; Mercury—mustard seed; Venus—small marshmallow; Earth—small marshmallow; Mars—peppercorn; Jupiter—small grapefruit or large orange; Saturn—medium-sized orange or small apple; Uranus—large cherry tomato or radish; Neptune—small cherry tomato, cherry, or small radish; Pluto—poppy seed.

Our Solar System

List the planets in our solar system in the order they appear, starting with the planet closest to the sun. Read about the different sizes of the planets and how they compare to each other. Use planet representations such as seeds, balls, or fruit to see how the planets compare to each other in size. **Draw a diagram in your journal that shows the planets orbiting the sun. In the diagram, show how the planets compare to one another in size.**

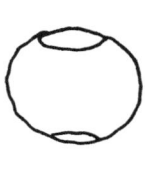

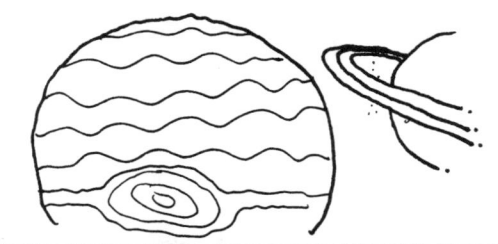

Solar System, Weather, & Rocks and Minerals

Life on Jupiter

Read about Jupiter. Find out what its daily temperatures are and other things we have learned about it from satellites. Pretend that Earth has become overpopulated, and that you have volunteered to move to Jupiter. How would you have to adapt to living on this large planet? **Write a story in your journal that tells what happens to you, beginning with your arrival on the planet.** Use your imagination, but base your story on what you read about Jupiter.

Life on Mercury

You are an astronaut who has been assigned to live on Mercury for one year. You will be in charge of a space station there. **Read about Mercury, then write a story in your journal about the adaptations you have to make to live there.** How could you grow vegetables and fruits? What would you do for exercise? How could you beat the heat on this, the closest planet to the sun? **Write about what it would be like to run the space station for a year.** Use information from your notes on Mercury and your knowledge of plant life, energy, and other areas of science as you write.

The Milky Way

Galaxies have different shapes. Find out what shape our galaxy has, and draw a picture of it. Why do you think it is called the Milky Way galaxy? There are different folk tales about the Milky Way. Sometimes people have imagined that it is like a path from heaven to Earth. **In your journal, write your own legend about the Milky Way.**

Ancient People and an Eclipse

Long ago, before it was known that the earth is round and that it orbits the sun, people didn't know what was happening during an eclipse. Some thought the gods were angry. Others may have seen it as a warning of something to come.

Pretend you are an average person living long ago. You can choose to be an Aztec or Maya Indian, a Greek, an Egyptian, or someone from another ancient civilization. Keep a diary as this person. **Write an entry in your diary (your journal) on the day of a solar eclipse. Write about what you think is happening, whether you are afraid or not, and how your friends and family react.**

© Carson-Dellosa Publ. CD-7317 *Solar System, Weather, & Rocks and Minerals*

Eclipses

There are two different types of eclipses: solar and lunar. They happen when the light from the sun is blocked by the moon or the earth. Does a solar eclipse happen during the day or the night? **Diagram in your journal what happens during a solar eclipse and then what happens during a lunar eclipse. Explain how they are similar and how they are different.**

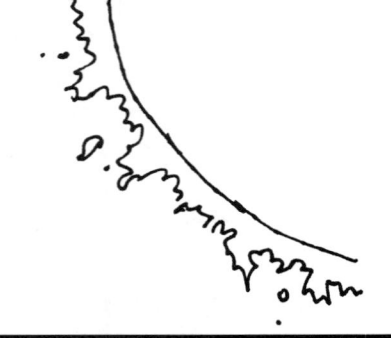

The Man in the Moon

There are many myths about the moon. Often, people say there is a man in the moon because its craters make shadows that sometimes look like a face. Have you ever seen a face when you have looked at the full moon? Find out what caused these moon craters. **In your journal, write a paragraph about the origin of these craters.**

In your journal, draw pictures of the faces of the man in the moon in both the full and crescent phases. You can draw what you really see when you look at the moon, or you can create something on your own. **Write a poem about the man in the moon to go with your pictures. Try to describe the moon in both phases, full and crescent, in your poem.**

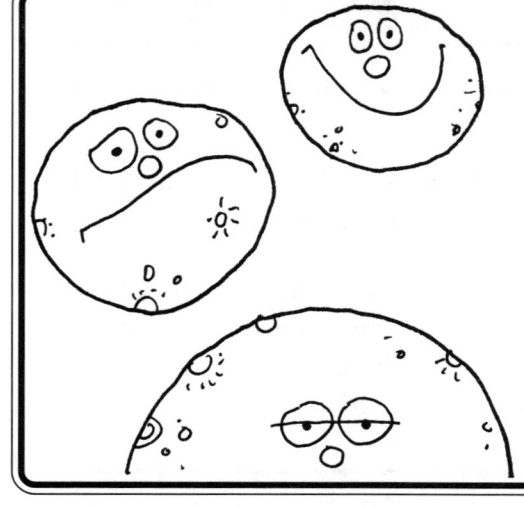

Making a Moon Myth

Write a myth in your journal about the moon. Your myth should tell why the moon is full and bright sometimes and why it is only a tiny sliver in the sky other times. Is the moon angry, sad, afraid, or something else? Is that what makes it change? Is someone using the moon in some way? What makes it grow back? What happens to the missing part? Where does it go during the new moon phase when we don't see a moon at night? Whatever your story suggests as reasons for the moon's changes, explain why it all happens. **Draw cartoon pictures for your story.**

Solar System, Weather, & Rocks and Minerals

What Happened to the Moon?

Sometimes the moon looks round and full. Other times, it looks like a tiny sliver. What happens to it? Some nights, there is no moon in the sky. Why does it seem to disappear? **Find the answers in the library, and write a story about it in your journal.** In your story, explain how the moon looks different depending on its position, the Earth's position, and the sun's position in the sky. While you read your story to the class, work with two friends (one acting as the sun and one acting as the Earth) to dramatize why the moon appears to change.

Moon Phases

The moon orbits the earth. As it does, it passes through different phases, depending on your location on earth and the moon's location in relation to the earth and sun. Look at pictures to see the phases of the moon as it cycles from full moon to full moon. Once a week, look outside and draw the moon as it appears. **The next week, transfer the drawing onto a calendar that you have drawn in your journal.**

Continue keeping a record of the moon's phases until you have observed and recorded the moon completing one full cycle. **Write a paragraph in your journal explaining what appears to happen to the moon as it passes through its cycle.** Explain why it looks different to us on earth even though it hasn't really changed.

Cloudy Pictures teacher's directions—Provide your students with tempera paints or pastels and blue construction paper for the Cloudy Pictures activity below.

Cloudy Pictures

Observe different types of clouds either in books or outside. Paint pictures of the clouds using tempera paints or pastels. Make several different paintings and label the types of clouds shown in your paintings. **List the types in your journal and write a brief description of each.**

© Carson-Dellosa Publ. CD-7317   *Solar System, Weather, & Rocks and Minerals*

Cloud Watching

Keep a chart in your science journal to track the daily cloud conditions for one week. Make a chart that lists the days of the week, and the cloud types, such as *cirrus*, *cumulus*, *stratus*, etc. Check the conditions at the same time each day. If possible, try to check the cloud conditions in the morning and the afternoon. Put a check mark beside the cloud types you see each day. At the end of the week, count the number of times you saw each cloud type. Which type did you see most often? Which type did you see least often?

Shape-Shifting Cloud

You are a magic cloud that is able to change its shape into anything. **Write a story in your journal as the shape-shifting cloud.** What shapes do you become, and why? Where do you go as you move across the sky? Do you sometimes carry rain or snow? Tell what it is like to be a cloud that can control its shape. How do people or animals react to you?

Cloud Clues

Clouds have scientific names. It can be hard to remember which type looks puffy and which looks wispy. **Make a list of the types of clouds, write a short description of each one in your journal, and indicate the type of weather each cloud represents.**

See if you can find an example outside or a picture of each type of cloud. Of what does each type remind you? Some people think of puffy mountains when they see cumulus clouds, for example. **Draw a picture in your journal of each cloud type. Beside each drawing, draw what that kind of cloud reminds you of, and label it.** For instance, if you draw a puffy mountain for cumulus clouds, you would label it *cumulus cloud = mountain*.

Solar System, Weather, & Rocks and Minerals

Visible Wind

Have you ever seen the wind? Sometimes we see trees and flowers sway when the wind passes through them, or clothes flapping in the wind as they hang from a clothesline. What does the wind really look like? **Draw a picture in your journal of what you think the wind would look like if you could suddenly see it. Write a poem about the wind and what it does as it blows during the day.**

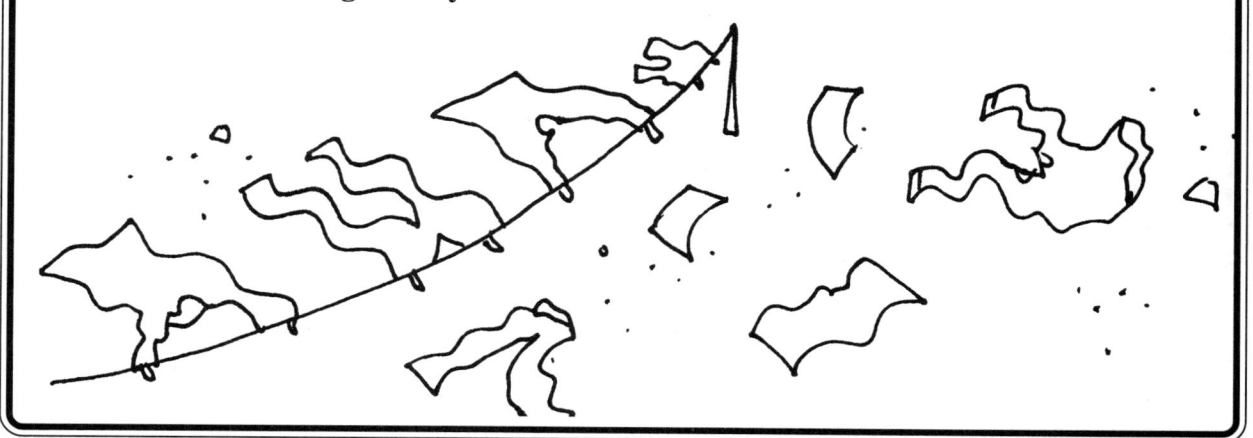

Daily Weather Conditions

Keep a chart in your science journal to track the daily weather conditions. Make a table to record the daily temperature, the precipitation, and the sky conditions. Check the weather at the same time every day. If you can, record the morning and the afternoon conditions every day. For example, at 9:00 a.m. every morning, read an outdoor thermometer and record the temperature, check a rain or snow gauge to see if there has been precipitation, and draw a symbol that represents the sky conditions (sunny, partly sunny, cloudy, foggy, etc.). Keep the chart for at least one month.

Forecasting the Weather

Look at a daily weather conditions chart, such as in a newspaper, and try to find some patterns in the weather. What happens to the temperature before a rainy day? What temperature or weather condition trends do you see from week to week?

Write a paragraph in your journal about the patterns you see in the weather, then use the patterns to try to forecast the next day's weather. On a separate chart in your journal, write what you think the temperature and sky conditions will be. If you think it will rain or snow, predict how much. The next day, check how accurate your forecast was. Continue to forecast the weather for at least two weeks, keeping a record of how successful each prediction was. As time passes, do your forecasts become more accurate? Why or why not?

The Water Cycle

The amount of water on the earth is the same now as it was millions of years ago. Nature recycles the water in a process called the *water cycle*. **In your journal, write a letter to a friend explaining the water cycle. Draw a diagram of the water cycle to help your friend understand how it works.** Explain why the water your friend drinks at the water fountain could be the same water that a dinosaur drank millions of years ago.

Rain Gauge teacher directions—Provide an ample supply of materials for students to assemble their own rain gauge designs. Materials can include 2-liter bottles, milk jugs, rulers, glass or plastic jars, masking tape, and other general craft supplies.

Rain Gauge

Think of how you can measure the amount of rain that falls during a day or week. Sometimes, just a little rain falls, while other times as much as an inch may fall. A rain gauge is a container that lets you collect and measure rainfall amounts. **In your journal, design a rain gauge to measure the precipitation.** Make the gauge and try it out. How reliable is it? **Record any improvements that you make to it and why you made the changes.**

Water and the Earth

Water covers about three-fourths of the Earth's surface. That means only about one-fourth of the earth is land on which we can live. Imagine you are an explorer looking for places people can live because the land has become too crowded. Read about wet suits and scuba gear to find out how people might adapt to live under water. **Write a story in your journal that tells about an imaginary undersea place you find on your explorations. Tell why the place is perfect for people. How will they build underwater houses, and how will they adapt to living under water?**

Solar System, Weather, & Rocks and Minerals   © Carson-Dellosa Publ. CD-7317

Buying Water

Without realizing it, people buy a lot of water that they don't drink in things like packaged food and household chemicals. People also pay a lot for drinks that have a high percentage of water in them. Read the labels of foods, drinks, and household products (such as shampoo). Keep a record of the product name and where water is in the list of ingredients. Sometimes, water will be listed first; this means water is the main ingredient. Other times, water will be listed farther down the list, meaning there is more of the first ingredients than there is of water.

Compare fruit juice concentrate to canned fruit juice or frozen vegetables to canned vegetables. Compare powdered household chemicals with similar liquid products. **In your journal, draw some conclusions about which products are the best value for the money.**

Walking on Water

Water has a special property called *surface tension*. This tension is why some things float. It also lets some types of insects and spiders walk on water. Read about surface tension. **Take notes in your journal as you read. Draw a pair of special shoes that would let people walk on water without breaking the surface tension. Explain your water shoes in an advertisement designed to sell the shoes to people. Include an illustration of the shoes.**

My Favorite Season

Which season is your favorite? **In your journal, name your favorite season and list at least ten reasons why you like it best.** Think about the weather, the activities you do, the way plants look, and how the season compares to your least-favorite season. Look at your list and number the reasons. Put a 1 by the most important reason you like that season, a 2 next to the second-most important reason, and so on down the list. **Write a story about your favorite season, and include at least five of your top reasons for liking the season.**

Adapting to the Seasons

Think of the changes that seasons bring. People adapt by wearing different amounts of clothing and using a heater or an air conditioner to make buildings comfortable. Plants and animals do not have those luxuries. Think of the adaptations plants and animals make as the seasons change. **Write in your journal about some of the changes made by mammals, reptiles, and birds. Also, write about the adaptations made by trees, flowers, and other plants.** What would happen if we did not have spring and fall? How would it affect the plants and animals if hot summer days suddenly turned into cold winter ones?

Seasonal Folk Tales

Think of the seasons as if they were people. Imagine what winter would look like, and what the other seasons would look like. **In your journal, draw pictures of the seasons, then write a folk tale about the seasons as characters.** You could write a story about why we have seasons or a story about the personalities and relationships the seasons might have and how they cause the weather to change.

Earth's Orbit and the Seasons

Why do you think we have different seasons throughout the year? Read about the tilt of the earth and how it affects the seasons as the earth orbits the sun. Why do we have summer when people in another hemisphere are having winter? Some places are always warm; find out where they are and why they do not have cool temperatures. **Write a paragraph in your journal that explains the reason we have seasons.**

The Ozone Layer

The *ozone layer* is a protective layer of gases around the earth. It shields the earth from the sun's harmful ultraviolet rays. Without the ozone layer, the harsh ultraviolet rays could destroy all plant life on which animal life depends. The ozone layer has been fairly consistent throughout the earth's history until recently, when people began creating chemicals that destroy the ozone layer. Find out what some of these chemicals are. Find out what people can use instead of these chemicals. Pretend you are trying to persuade the people in the world to save the ozone layer. **Write in your journal what you would say to people to convince them.**

Solar System, Weather, & Rocks and Minerals

Fixing a Hole

The ozone layer has some holes so large in it that people are trying to stop destroying it. Pretend that you are a scientist who has been hired to fix the holes. **Write a story in your journal that tells what your plan is, how you will follow it, any problems you might have, and whether you think you will be successful or not.** Use your imagination and your knowledge of how some chemicals have made the holes to think of ways you could fix the holes.

Adapting to the Sun's Radiation

Imagine that people didn't care about the ozone layer and that they finally destroyed it. Plants and animals are dying from exposure to the strong ultraviolet radiation from the sun. The earth will soon look like Mars and other barren planets if something is not done. **Write a story in your journal that tells what the survivors do to stay alive.** Tell about the houses and towns they build, and how they protect plants and animals. Tell what they do to shield their fields so they can grow food to eat. They cannot save every type of animal on earth, so they must select which ones to help. Tell which ones they selected and why they chose those animals.

Acid Rain

Acid rain is caused by pollution. People can remove the harmful chemicals from acid rain, but plants and animals cannot. This means the plants and animals take in the pollution with the water, and it can make them so sick that they eventually die. Some animals have to live in ponds that receive a lot of acid rain. Find out the sources of pollution that cause acid rain. **In your journal, design some advertisements that tell about acid rain and its effects. Have the ads make people aware of the problem, as well as what they can do to solve the problem. Make one advertisement for a magazine, one for television, and one for radio.**

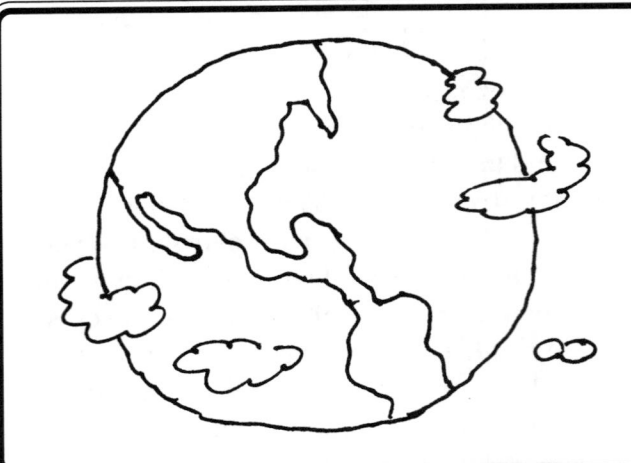

The Earth Is a Rock

Of what is the earth made? **In your journal, draw a diagram of the *crust*, *mantle*, and *core* of the earth.** Read about how volcanoes are formed and what makes earthquakes. **Take notes in your journal as you read, and then write a story about when the earth was new with active volcanoes and frequent earthquakes. Describe what it must have been like.**

Earth's Rocks

The earth contains all sorts of rocks. There are three basic types of rock—*sedimentary*, *igneous*, and *metamorphic*. **Write these three types in your journal, and then find a few facts about each one and list them, too.** How is each type of rock formed? Go on a rock hunt and try to find an example of each type. Use a rock identification book to help you.

Prehistoric Life on Earth

Millions of years ago life was very different on earth. Dinosaurs once roamed the earth, and the earth looked quite different. Pretend you are a scientist who is trying to prove that dinosaurs once existed. How do we know that? What records can you use? **Write about how you could prove that dinosaurs once existed.**

Solar System, Weather, & Rocks and Minerals © Carson-Dellosa Publ. CD-7317

Fossil Records

Fossils are very important because they let us see how life and the Earth have changed over time. Find out how fossils were formed. What sorts of fossils do you think mankind might leave behind if we became extinct? Use clay to make some "fossil" prints that future intelligent life could find as a record of our existence. **In your journal, label and draw a sketch of each fossil you make, and write a short paragraph that tells why you chose that particular item to turn into part of our fossil history.**

Gems and Other Special Stones

Some minerals are rare or difficult to find and possess great beauty. Such minerals are considered *gemstones*. **Look up this term in an encyclopedia and list in your journal the names of several gemstones.** Back before people used coins and paper for money, they traded things like stones. Create a money system based on gemstones. Which stones would be the most valuable? Which ordinary stone could represent our penny? Which rare, special gemstone could represent the value of our $100 bill? Think about the rarity, the mining difficulty, or the special colors of the stones when you make your system. **In your journal, make a diagram that shows the stones in your money system and their value. Explain your system, telling why you selected each stone for the specified value.**

Finding Minerals in Products teacher directions—You might want to supply the students with a box of products that they can use for the rock activity below. Read the labels to make sure the ones you supply have the indicated mineral in them. Many medicines such as cold and stomach remedies have talc in them; salt—a form of halite—is in many products; and mica is in some eye shadows and other makeup.

Finding Minerals in Products

We use minerals all the time and do not even realize it. Minerals are in many common things. For instance, *quartz* is used to make glass, and a steel pin has *hematite* in it. Try to find minerals in at least four common products. **In your journal, list the products and the minerals they contain.** If you can find more than four, list them as well.

The Solar System, Weather, and Rocks and Minerals Supplementary Activities

"Sharing Space" Bulletin Board

To learn more about the galaxy, let the students create a "Sharing Space" bulletin board. Have the students photocopy (and enlarge) and cut out the Earth, moon, and star patterns found on page 57 and the constellation patterns found on pages 58 and 59. You can then let the students arrange the patterns to create a bulletin board.

1. **Read some star myths that tell how different constellations were formed.** For instance, some Greek myths say the constellation Orion is a great hunter. Native American legend says Orion is a warrior who carries the sun. Some books you might share with the class are *The Constellations,* by Lloyd Motz and Carol Nathanson (Doubleday, 1988), and *The Constellations: How They Came to Be,* by Roy A. Gallant (Four Winds Press, 1979).

    After sharing some star stories with the class, ask the students to write a legend about the constellations they will create on the bulletin board. **As extensions, they can write myths in their science journals about the seasons, the arrangement and names of the planets, and about day and night.**

2. **Look at photographs of actual constellations and ask the students to match each photograph with the corresponding pattern from pages 58 and 59.** A guide such as *Peterson's First Guides: Astronomy,* by Jay M. Pasachoff (Houghton Mifflin, 1988), will show the students how the stars are arranged in various constellations. Let the students pick one constellation to display on a separate piece of poster board or bulletin board. You might find it best for the class to put up a different constellation each week. The students can make a two-dimensional constellation display by arranging white push pins on a bulletin board covered with dark paper and winding white yarn around the pins to outline the constellation. Ask two or three students to work together to create the constellation display. **Encourage the students to draw pictures of the selected constellation in their science journals.** Another idea is to ask small groups of students to create new constellations, complete with star names and legend. This is a challenge you can present, and then let the class work on for a day or two. The groups of students can then display each new constellation on the bulletin board and tell its accompanying story.

Field Trip

Take the class on a field trip to a planetarium where the students can see how the planets and stars appear to "move" across the sky. They will also be able to see a simulated night sky without any buildings, trees, or mountains to obstruct their view. **Have the students write about their planetarium experiences in their science journals.**

Earth, Moon, and Star Patterns

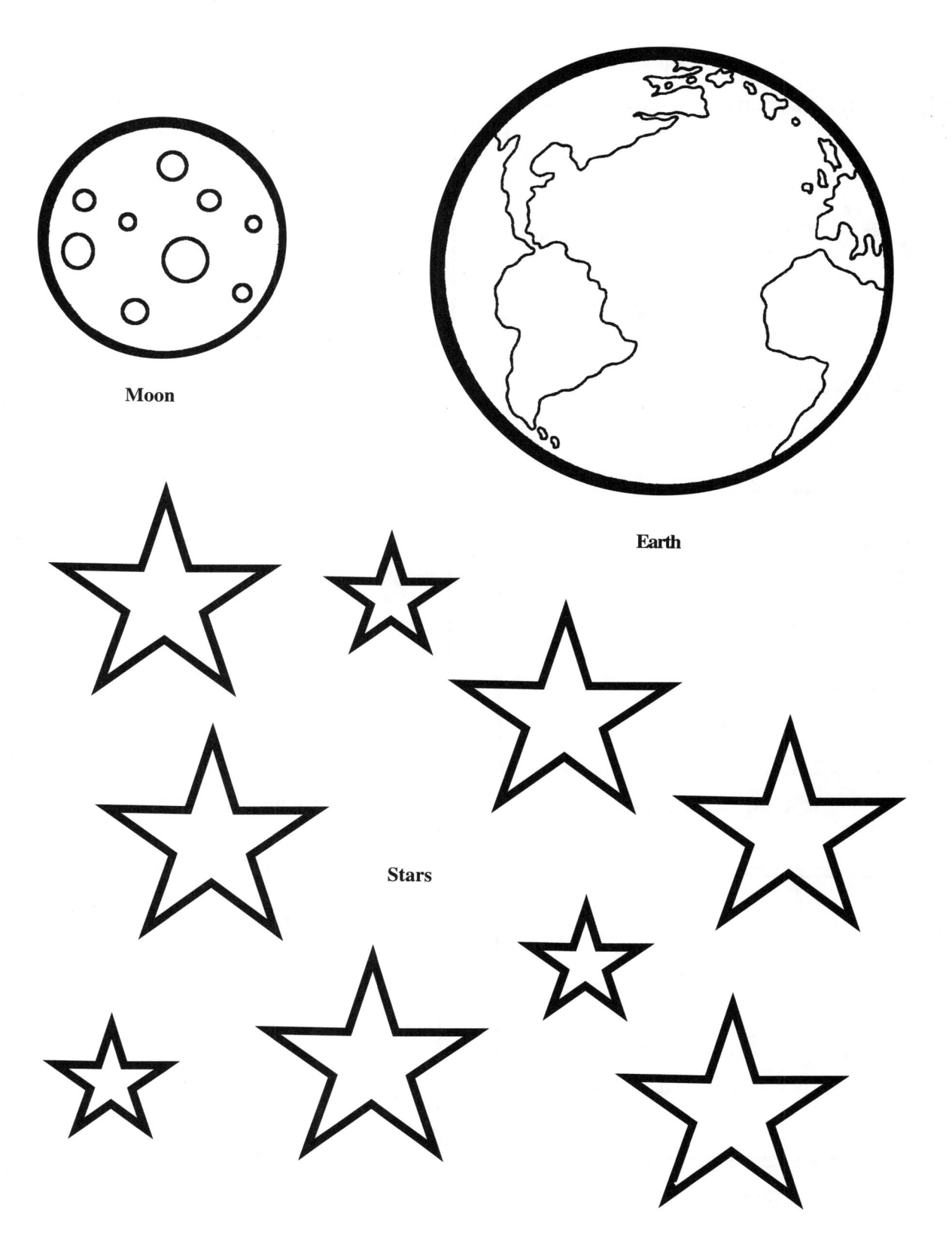

Moon

Earth

Stars

© Carson-Dellosa Publ. CD-7317

Solar System, Weather, & Rocks and Minerals

Constellation Patterns

Reproduce and display the constellations on this and the following page on your bulletin board.

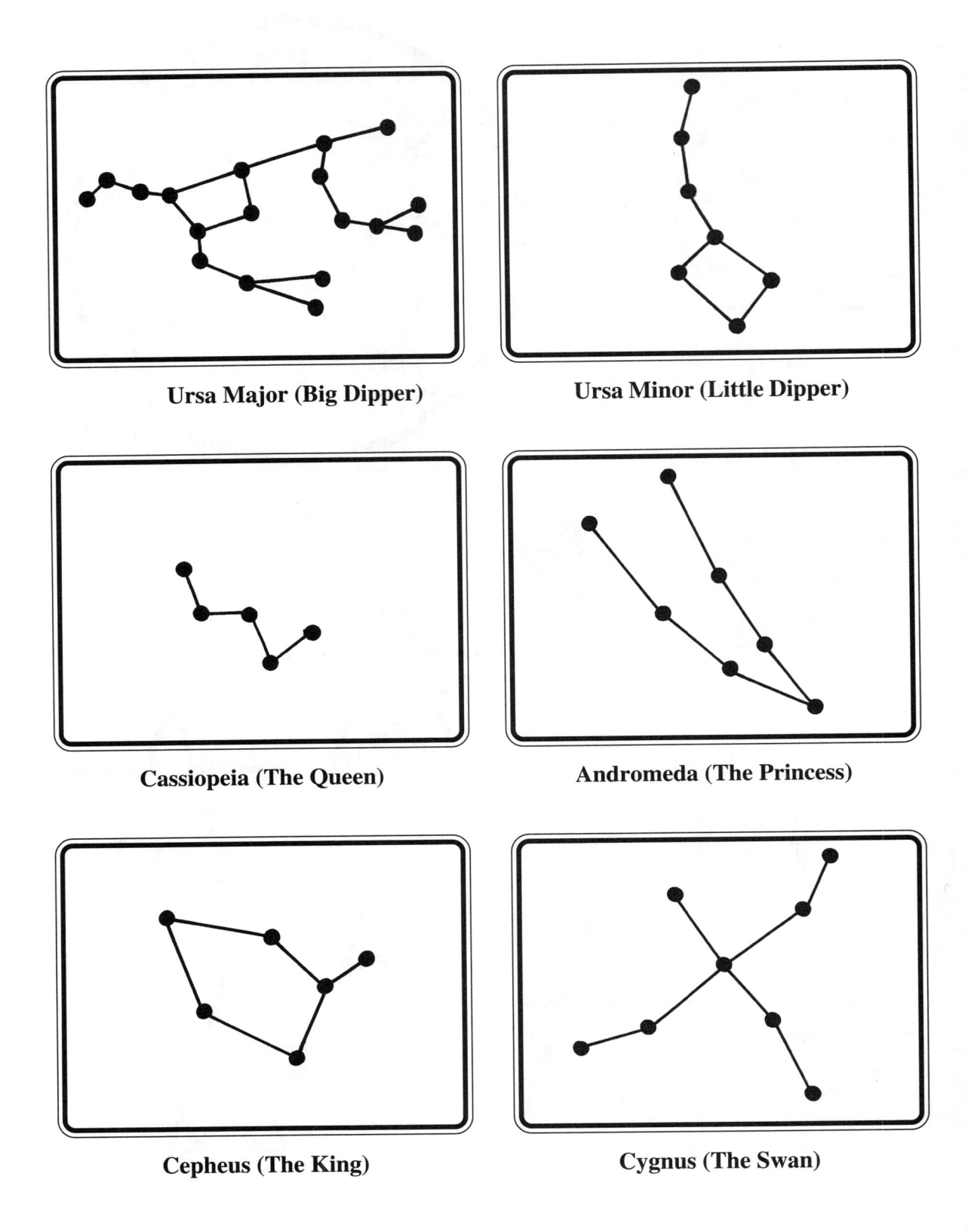

Ursa Major (Big Dipper)

Ursa Minor (Little Dipper)

Cassiopeia (The Queen)

Andromeda (The Princess)

Cepheus (The King)

Cygnus (The Swan)

Solar System, Weather, & Rocks and Minerals © Carson-Dellosa Publ. CD-7317

Constellation Patterns (continued)

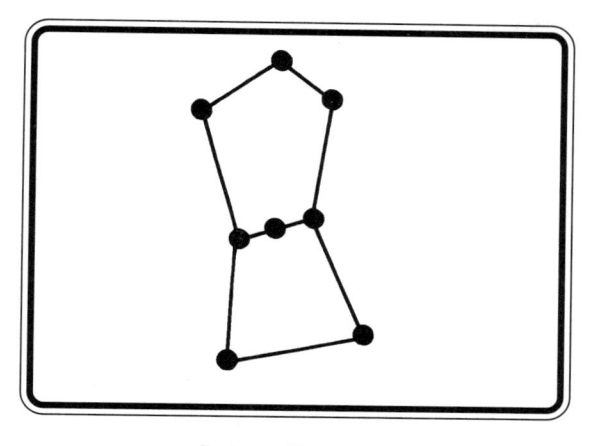

Orion (The Hunter)

Leo (The Lion)

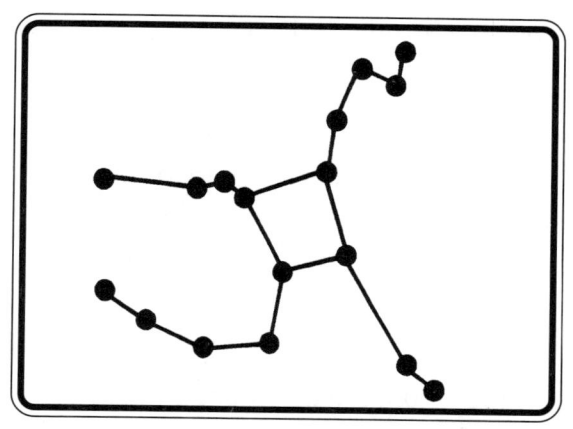

Hercules (The Strong Man)

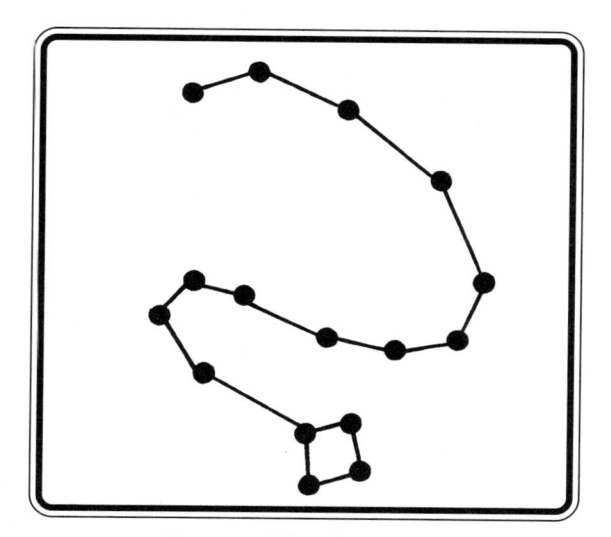

Draco (The Dragon)

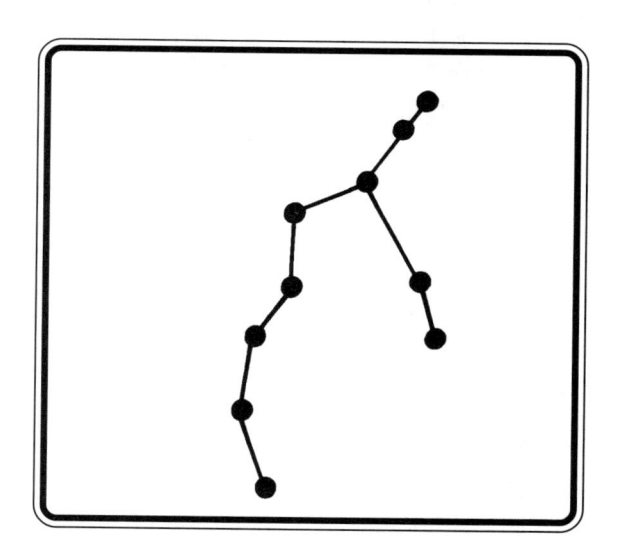

Perseus (The Hero)

© Carson-Dellosa Publ. CD-7317

Solar System, Weather, & Rocks and Minerals

Travel Agency

The following activity can help your students understand that science is helpful even in nonscientific careers. For instance, the students will learn that it can be important to understand the varying climate and weather of different regions of their state or country when traveling.

To begin this learning segment, explain that the class is opening a travel agency. Tell the students their mission is to encourage people to visit state and national parks. Ask the class to decide which state and federal parks their agency will promote, and then to create committees to conduct research on each park. **Instruct the committees to use their science journals to record the information for their presentation:**

1. **Learn about the location of the park:** What is the climate within the park? What is the terrain like, and what surrounds the park? How is the park special or different from other parks in the state or nation?

2. **Find out what habitats are in the park:** What plants and animals live within each habitat? Are there any plants or animals unique to the park, and if so, where and why are they found there? How do the habitats blend, creating the park's ecosystem? What are the water and food sources in the park?

3. **Find out what the park offers:** Are there trails for walking, biking, horseback riding, or backpacking? What types of facilities does the park offer visitors: camp sites, cabins, or lodge rooms? Is there a place to fish, and if so, are special permits required? Why or why not? What other recreational activities does the park offer visitors?

4. **Learn about the landscape:** What type of landscape is there—mountains, desert, hills, or something else? What is special about the landscape? What sorts of rocks are found there? How does the landscape affect the wildlife that is found there?

5. **Organize the information:** Work together to see how the facts and interesting aspects of a park go together. Figure out how to combine all the information from all the parks into one brochure for your agency. Think about how to arrange the information in a brochure to entice people to visit. Design a sketch of the brochure's layout, so you can see how to put the information together.

6. **Create the brochure:** Write the information as you would if it were to be published for the public. Add illustrations, diagrams, or other interesting visual effects.

7. **Write a sales pitch:** What would you say to someone who came to your travel agency for help in planning a vacation? How would you promote the parks your agency researched? Write a sales pitch to persuade someone that a park in your brochure is a perfect vacation spot.

8. **Present the information to the rest of the class:** Draw travel posters to display around the room. Show the class sample pages of the brochure, pictures from the park, etc.

Solar System, Weather, & Rocks and Minerals

Rocks and Minerals Bulletin Board

To make a Rocks and Minerals display, first divide a bulletin board into three horizontal or vertical sections. Label each section with one of the following headings: *igneous, sedimentary,* and *metamorphic.* Ask the class to help you write a description of each type of rock. Post the descriptions under the headings.

Purchase small samples of the three types of rock from a nature or educational store and glue them onto poster board. When the glue is dry, attach the poster board onto the bulletin board under the appropriate heading.

Have the students list as many different rocks and minerals as they can. Let them print the rock and mineral names onto colored paper and then place the names in the appropriate section of the bulletin board. Be sure they list some igneous and sedimentary samples that become metamorphic rocks. For instance, granite (igneous) becomes marble (metamorphic) under intense heat and pressure, and shale (sedimentary) becomes slate (metamorphic) under intense heat and pressure. Slate, in turn, can become phyllite, schist, and finally gneiss. Additionally, some rocks look different depending on how they are formed; for instance, igneous pumice and obsidian are products of the same liquid rock, but look very different. Show the class samples of these, if possible, and have them draw examples for the bulletin board.

"Melt Down" Game

Discuss how crystals are formed as molten rock cools. Explain that if there is plenty of space between the particles of molten rock and the molten rock cools slowly, the crystals that are formed are large and properly structured. If there is little space or the rock cools too quickly, the crystals are small and often irregular.

As a follow-up game that demonstrates how crystals form, ask the students to form two lines facing each other. Tell each student to reach across and grab the hands of two different people in the other line; tell students to be sure not to grab the hands of people who are directly across from them if possible. Tell the students to note where they are standing in the line and to note whose hands they are holding.

When you say, "Melt down!" the students should drop their hands and move around the room as if they were free-flowing molten rock. When you begin to count down from ten, they are to re-form the exact "crystal" structure they just made. Give the "Melt down" order, and let the students spread out and move about. Slowly count down from ten and let the students re-form their "crystal" shape. Repeat the "Melt down!" game, only this time count down from ten *quickly,* so the students will end up in a jumbled mess. Play the game several times. Examine some real crystals afterward. Ask the class which crystals took more time and space to form.

Mining for Minerals

Ask the students to write a few sentences in their journals that explain the differences between a rock and a mineral. Then, have the students mine for fake minerals. All you need is a bag of chocolate-chip and nut cookies, some tongue depressors or craft sticks, and some paper towels to cover the work areas. Tell the class to pretend the cookie is a rock and to try to separate the minerals (the chips and nuts) from the earth (the cookie). Have the students compare how many chips and nuts they found in their cookie mines with the numbers found by classmates around them, and record these numbers. **Have them describe the mining experience in their journals. Discuss what kind of difficulties a geologist might have while mining for minerals. Allow the students to eat their "minerals" when the activity has been completed.**

Science Review Exercises

The following activities can help reinforce the material the class has learned. You can adapt these exercises for a specific topic or section, or use them as a general review of scientific concepts.

Silly Sentences

Make up silly sentences that contradict science facts and let the students figure out what is wrong with them (see the examples below). At first, have the class work together to explain what is wrong with the sentences. Later, you might want to write a silly sentence on the chalkboard and let the students write what the problem is and how to correct it in their journals.

Another way to make a game with the silly sentences is to write them on cards. Have each student write a silly sentence on the front of an index card and put an explanation of why it is wrong on the back. After you have collected all the cards from the class, shuffle them and let the students take turns drawing a card, reading it aloud, and explaining what makes it silly. Students can check their answers by looking at the explanation on the backs of the cards. The Silly Sentences activity could serve as a good review for true/false questions on an exam. Use the following silly sentences to get started:

- The sun froze the pond last night.
- A school of minnows swam across the deep blue sky.
- An Aspen tree's leaves turn yellow in spring before they fall off.
- The ozone layer around the sun was getting smaller.
- My skin was burned by the moon last night.
- It was a hot, snowy day.
- My food web tastes great!
- The chicken laid a fossil.

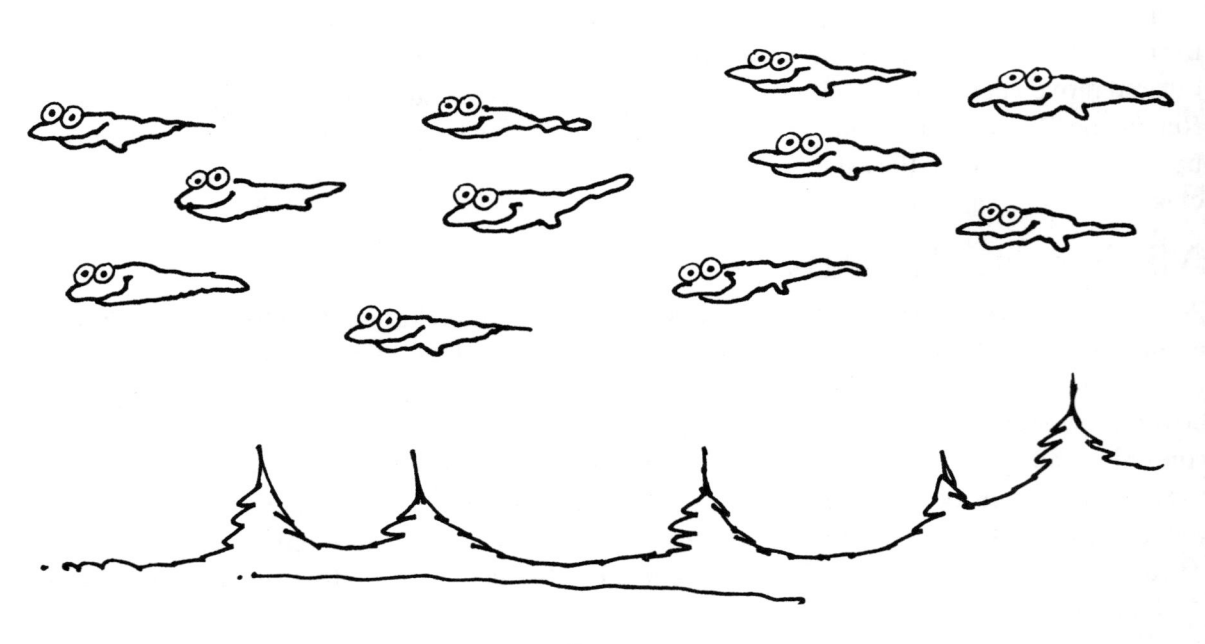

Scientific Puzzles

The activities below can be a fun way to reinforce many of the scientific terms the students have learned. Make photocopies of the students' finished puzzles so everyone can try them. While the students are creating their puzzles, emphasize the importance of spelling the terms correctly!

1. **Ask each student to make a crossword puzzle that uses at least ten scientific words, such as** *mammal, igneous, dicot, endothermic, eclipse,* **etc.** The student should write a clue for each word in his puzzle. Each student should also make an answer key for his puzzle on another sheet of paper. (It may be helpful for the students to see some examples of crossword puzzles before beginning.)
2. **Have each student create a hidden-word puzzle that has at least twenty scientific words hidden in it.** Ask the students to list the hidden words beside the puzzle. Tell the students to make a separate answer key that has the words circled. The hidden word search activity below may help the students get started. The hidden words can be listed across, down, or diagonally.

Hidden Word Search

CELL	DECIDUOUS	FLOWERS	INSECTS	SEED
CHRYSALIS	DICOT	FOOD WEB	LIGHT	SOLAR SYSTEM
CONIFEROUS	ECLIPSE	GALAXY	METAMORPHIC	SOUND
CUMULUS	ECTOTHERMIC	HYPOTHESIS	MONOCOT	SPECTRUM
CURRENT	ENDOTHERMIC	IGNEOUS	OZONE	SYMMETRY

S	G	F	L	C	H	R	Y	S	A	L	I	S	V	T	E
O	H	A	S	I	E	R	P	F	A	M	L	S	O	N	D
L	Y	I	L	C	G	N	Z	W	B	Y	J	C	O	L	E
A	P	S	N	A	E	H	D	V	X	C	I	Z	L	H	C
R	O	Y	L	S	X	C	T	O	I	D	O	E	H	C	I
S	T	M	S	S	E	Y	L	M	T	G	C	S	O	H	D
Y	H	M	W	N	A	C	R	I	C	H	I	K	E	K	U
S	E	E	S	A	X	E	T	F	P	U	E	D	X	N	O
T	S	T	S	R	H	T	C	S	O	S	M	R	Q	N	U
E	I	R	S	T	N	S	S	T	S	O	E	U	M	S	S
M	S	Y	O	E	R	U	O	D	B	O	D	S	L	I	G
M	Q	T	R	E	O	C	Q	A	F	X	U	W	E	U	C
C	C	R	W	E	O	K	S	J	J	U	J	N	E	E	S
E	U	O	N	N	S	P	E	C	T	R	U	M	D	B	D
C	L	G	O	R	Y	C	O	N	I	F	E	R	O	U	S
F	I	M	A	H	M	E	T	A	M	O	R	P	H	I	C

Answer Key

"What Would Happen If?" Skits

First, write some "What Would Happen If?" skit starters (listed below) on index cards. Explain to the students that they will work in teams to show what might happen if the situations on the cards occurred. Tell the students to use science theory and facts when they make up their skits. Instruct the students to write the skits in their science journals. You may want to let a different group tackle a skit each day, or you may want to devote a whole afternoon to this playful, but thought-provoking, review. Make up other questions to write on the index cards to enhance the topics the class is currently studying in science

1. **Divide the class into teams of performers.** Let one team choose a "What Would Happen If?" skit starter from a bag or box. Give the group a set amount of time, around ten minutes, to work together to create a skit that shows what might happen if the situation on the card really occurred. The students will have to draw on their knowledge of the topic and work together quickly to make up the skit. The goal is for them to use knowledge they already have, rather than spend time conducting research.

2. **Halfway through the allotted time, ring a bell or give some other signal so the group will know how much remaining time they have.** Use the same signal to conclude their preparation period, and then have them present their skit.

3. **The students who are not involved in preparing a skit can work on a journal idea from this book.** This can help them continue their science focus and keep the classroom quiet so the skit team can concentrate. You could have the students respond to the journal leading questions found on page 3, answering them in respect to the current unit.

4. **Make your own "What Would Happen If?" skit starters related to the units the class is studying or has finished.** You could keep adding to the bag or box of questions, so the students may get a card on a unit completed months earlier. This will help them review and learn the concepts you teach, rather than just memorize them short-term for unit tests. Some skit starters you might use are listed below:

   - What would happen if the sun suddenly burned out?
   - What would happen if water froze from the bottom instead of the top?
   - What would happen if all the water on earth dried up?
   - What would happen if the ozone layer suddenly disappeared?
   - What would happen if people could no longer use electricity?
   - What would happen if dinosaurs lived on the earth again?
   - What would happen if insects were no longer attracted to flowers?

Science Review Exercises